LIBRARY OF THE EARLY CIVILIZATIONS
EDITED BY PROFESSOR STUART PIGGOTT

The First Merchant Venturers

THE FIRST

THE ANC

IN

McGRAW-HILL BOOK

MERCHANT VENTURERS

IENT LEVANT

HISTORY AND COMMERCE

William Culican

c, 1

COMPANY · NEW YORK

913.39
CULICAN

DESIGNED AND PRODUCED BY THAMES AND HUDSON

CONTENTS

GENERAL EDITOR'S PREFACE

The ancient peoples of the Levant, that strip of westwards-facing coast bounding the eastern limits of the Mediterranean Sea, had like the country they inhabited a diversity of character and independent individuality contrasting with the uniformity of culture in Egypt or Mesopotamia, their neighbouring great states. The natural resources of the Levant, notably in timber and metal, and the long coast-line with its harbours, favoured the rise of sea-going mercantile communities, but we first see the natural resources being exploited by the great powers who had a long tradition of literate civilization behind them. The Egyptians to the south, and first the Sumerians and later the Assyrians to the east both needed timber for building purposes on a large scale, and precious metals were equally in demand in these prosperous societies.

Already by the later third millennium BC the 'Cedar Forest' of the Amanus and the 'Silver Mountain', probably in the Taurus, were established objectives for the Assyrian traders. The Forest was already legendary, for Gilgamesh and Enkidu had been there – 'they gazed at the mountain of cedars, the dwelling-place of the gods . . . the hugeness of the cedar tree rose in front of the mountain, its shade was beautiful, full of comfort; mountain and glade were green with brushwood'. And then, when Gudea was temple-building in Lagash, he 'made a path into the Cedar Mountain which nobody had entered before, he cut its cedars with great axes. . . . Like giant snakes, cedar rafts were floating down the river.'

Egyptians and Minoans too were concerned with the metal trade with the Levant, and we are soon in the world of active overseas trade which made possible the splendours of Solomon's palace and temple, 'wholly Phoenician in character', in the tenth century BC. The contacts and inter-relations of this time went beyond the confines of the Eastern Mediterranean, and the elaborate metal cauldrons on wheeled bases in the Temple, described in the First Book of Kings, have archaeological counterparts in Cyprus or, in smaller and simpler form, in Central and Northern Europe at this time as found in Czechoslovakia and Scandinavia.

Wherever remote Tarshish may have been in fact – that 'Timbuktu of antiquity' – Phoenician and Syro-Hittite art styles soon began to make their way westwards along the Mediterranean sea-ways, and with the establishment of first the North African and then the Iberian colonies from the later eighth century BC, Phoenician trade and settlement became firm facts in the west. Historical Tartessos dates from the late seventh century, and Carthaginian trade was extended through the Straits and up the Lusitanian coast, perhaps as far as Galicia, but not beyond. From the sixth century BC the 'situla art' developing round the head of the Adriatic is influenced not only by Greek Orientalizing motifs but, it seems likely, Phoenician modes as well: on the other hand, with the Carthaginians holding the Straits of Gibraltar, Greek trade with barbarian western Europe from the seventh century BC became concentrated on Massalia and her hinterland. Here in fact is the archaeology behind the poetry of Matthew Arnold's 'grave Tyrian trader' and 'the young light-hearted masters of the waves'.

Influence from the Levant were, it seems, constantly affecting and permeating the ancient world in almost every domain of human activity. 'The world of Homer had much in common with that of Ugarit', as reflected in the remarkable literary texts from Ras Shamra, and there must have been much exchange of thought, ideas and poetic techniques between these worlds. And finally of course we have to thank the Levant for alphabetic writing; the convention in which these words are printed goes back to the inscription on the Ahiram sarcophagus at Byblos, of the tenth century BC. Perhaps through the intermediary of the trading post at Al Mina this technique of representing the sounds of human speech reached Greece in the early eighth century, there to form the basis of all the subsequent phonetic codes of the western world.

STUART PIGGOTT

INTRODUCTION

The parts played by the ancient civilizations of the Nile Valley and the Mesopotamian river plains in the evolution of modern society are well known. Scarcely a year passes without some significant discovery which throws the origins of some part of our inheritance back beyond the Classical world. Indeed, whilst Greece, Rome and the Bible stand immediately behind our own religious and political concepts, we are constantly led to interpret their genius in the light they reflect from the Ancient Mediterranean and Near East. As early as 3000 BC the civilizations of the Nile and the Tigris were probably in sporadic touch, but down to the second millennium they were essentially parallel developments independent of each other. The area of their maximum contact was the Syrian and Palestinian seaboard, where in the second millennium BC Egyptians, Babylonians, Hurrians, Canaanites, Hittites, Minoans, Cypriots and Mycenaean Greeks were brought into one of the most formative relationships in human history, a relationship which although broken in the early first millennium by what has been called the 'Mediterranean Dark Age' continued to operate until the Persian Empire unified western Asia into a whole.

Trade exchanges in human societies can first be traced between the Mesolithic settled communities of the Near East. Amongst the Natufians of Palestine, shell beads produced on the coast found their way to settlements well inland. Anatolian obsidian and other foreign stones were prized for toolmaking by the Mesolithic people of Kurdistan. Such exchanges had increasing impact amongst Neolithic and Chalcolithic villagers, but organized commercial societies were a product of the advanced Bronze Age.

The trade relationships which sprang up in the early second millennium greatly accelerated the growth of civilization throughout the East Mediterranean basin. Crete, Mycenae and finally European Greece were drawn into the orbit of this trade, thus forming the channel by which much of the Oriental legacy was passed on. This small book aims to present to the student this interplay of cultures in the Levant in the light of archaeological research.

W. C.

CHRONOLOGICAL TABLE

BC		CYPRUS & ASIA MINOR	SYRO-PALESTINIAN COAST & N.SYRIA	CENTRAL PALESTINE	EGYPT	MESOPOTAMIA HISTORICAL LINKS
3000	EARLY		BYBLOS	GEZER · JERICHO MEGIDDO AI		2700 Contacts with Byblos 2600 Pharaoh Sneferu imports Lebanese cedar
			SMALL CITY STATES	OF WESTERN SEMITES		2350 Akkadian mention of 'Amurru' 2080 Gudea of Lagash imports Lebanese cedar
1900			NOMADIC SEMITES	FILTER INTO EGYPT ▶	1900 Nomad Semites pictured at Beni Hasan	
	MIDDLE	Rise of the Hittites	1900-1788 Cultural centres of Byblos & Ras Shamra Exchanges with Egypt c. 1730 HURRIAN STATES in N. Syria	The Patriarchal Age of Abraham, Isaac & Jacob		1730-1700 Archives at Mari show existence of Amorite kingdoms
			HYKSOS	INVASION		KASSITE DYNASTIES ▶
1550		INTENSIVE	TRADE OPENS BETWEEN	CYPRUS, PALESTINE AND	EGYPT	
	LATE (BRONZE AGE)		Rise of the MITANNI KINGDOMS	1500 Cultural focus shifts to Central Palestine	1525 Campaigns of Tuthmosis I against Hyksos	
			Penetration to Euphrates ◁			
				Siege of Megiddo 1468 ◁	1483-1463 Campaigns of Tuthmosis III in Palestine and Syria	
			Capture of Arvad ◁			
		Hittites intervene in Syro-Palestinian affairs	15th cent. King Idrimi of Alalakh	TELL EL-AMARNA LETTERS (EGYPT'S EMPIRE)	1440-1358 Amenophis II, III, IV dominate Syrian tribute to Egypt	
		Rise of ENKOMI	SPREAD OF MYCENAEAN INFLUENCE IN THE ENTIRE		LEVANT	
		Close contacts between Cyprus & Ugarit	1400-1250 Flourishing of Ras Shamra. Ugaritic Epics	Reciprocal Canaanite-Egyptian influences in Art and Religion		
		Hittite influence at Ugarit and interference in Syro-Palestinian affairs	1308, 1296 Battles at Kadesh ◁	Beginning of the Israelite settlement of Canaan	Seti I & Ramesses II	
1250	I (IRON AGE)	1200 INVASION OF	THE SEA PEOPLES		Repulsed by Ramesses III ▶	
				PHILISTINES SETTLE on S. Palestinian coast 1200-930 Subjugation of Canaan by Israelites Saul, David & Solomon		
		Rise of SYRO-HITTITE KINGDOMS	Rise of the Monarchy of Tyre		(EGYPTIAN INFLUENCE FALLS OFF)	1094 Tiglath-Pileser I in Syria
930			ARAMAEAN STATES IN N. SYRIA 814 Carthage founded?	Divided Monarchy in Israel		884-859 Ashurnasirpal
		Phoenician rule at Citium in Cyprus		684 Jerusalem attacked ◀		Sennacherib Ashurbanipal
	II		666 Tyre reduced ◀ 700-600 Phoenician expansion in West Mediterranean 609 Phoenician circum-navigation of Africa			
		Greek trade with Levant introduces oriental taste to the West		586 Jerusalem destroyed ◀		Nebuchadnezzar II

CHAPTER ONE

The Emergence of the Sea Peoples of the Levant

The story of the ancient communities of the Levant is broken in both the geographical and the historical sense, making it difficult for us to perceive any consistent patterns of culture common to them as a whole. The diversity between Palestine and Syria appears in early prehistoric times. The population of the North Syrian coast in the fifth millennium BC belonged in part to the users of the Tell Halaf painted pottery of northern Mesopotamia, which, along with the subsequent al'Ubaid ware (or its northern derivatives), forms the earliest widespread ceramic horizon. It is well represented at Ras Shamra, Tell Duruk, Jebleh and sites around Antioch as well as occurring at Mersin and elsewhere in south-east Anatolia. This horizon does not extend southwards into Palestine, where the local Chalcolithic cultures of Teleilat Ghassul and Beersheba were both perhaps derived from Transjordan and have only remote northern links. Certain correlations between Syria and Palestine are provided by the red-washed ware of Byblos type in Lebanon, but apart from here and at Ras Shamra very little is known about the earlier prehistoric phases of the coastal regions. The earliest settlers at Ras Shamra (about 6000 BC by C-14 dates) shared the dark-burnished neolithic pottery tradition

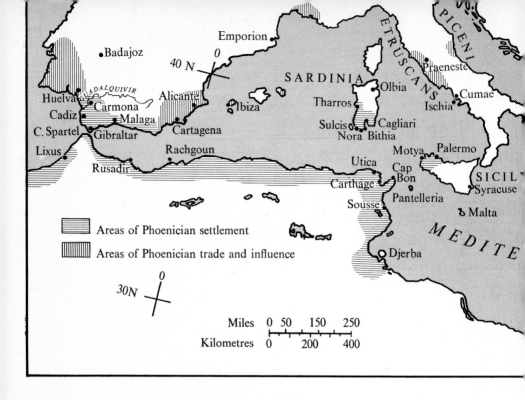

of the Syro-Cilician region and made tools of obsidian possibly obtained from central Anatolia. Their economy was entirely agricultural; what trade there was passed overland, and except for a little fishing, they were not equipped to trade by sea.

Throughout the ensuing Bronze Age the cities of Palestine and Syria remained the centres of small and independent kingdoms under petty rulers, whose allegiances were divided between Egypt, Babylonia and the great Hittite Empire. In such city-states, while individual genius might be fostered, the culture as a whole could not take on that characteristic form that we see for instance in the great kingdoms of Oriental antiquity.

Two main factors were responsible for this situation. Firstly, all the great powers looked upon Syria, and Palestine, its southern extension, merely as a sphere of influence, never important enough to merit colonization or colonial development. Secondly, the Levantine region

1 Phoenicians in the Mediterranean World

is itself one of great physical diversity. It was natural that the arid steppes which cross North Syria to the foothills of Kurdistan should attract incursions of northern peoples seeking *Lebensraum*, and that the narrow strip of fertile coastal land, cut off from the desert by the mountain ranges of Lebanon, should foster the growth of peaceful cities absorbed in market gardening and sea-borne trade. In the low hills of Jordania, settled in since the dawn of the use of metals and more fertile in antiquity than today, yet different communities arose, ancient peasant kingdoms such as that on the ancient site of Jericho, with strong fortified cities governing patches of plain. These communities were highly vulnerable from the south-western desert through which both Egyptian and Israelite conquerors came, just as the coastal cities were vulnerable to attack from the strong communities settled thickly in north-west Syria, in the foothills of the Amanus and the Amuq plain.

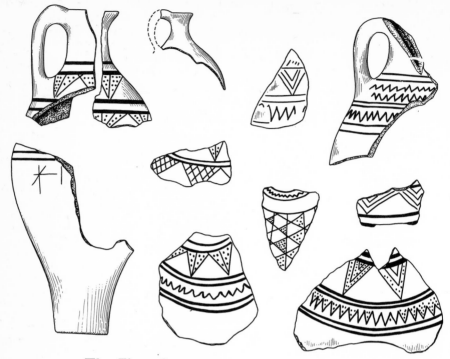

The First Contacts

The earliest recognizable trade relationships involving the Levant were consequent on the rise of wealthy dynasts in Egypt at a time corresponding with the Late Chalcolithic and Early Bronze Age I periods in Palestine. For the architectural ambitions of these new rulers Palestine and Syria could supply important materials which Egypt sadly lacked – timber and pitch, as well as being richer in metal resources, oils, essences and wax. In connection with the importation of these raw materials a few pottery vessels, probably containers of a refined oil, reached Egypt from Syria and Palestine and were buried in the Dynasty I tombs at Abydos. The precise origin of this Syro-Palestinian 'Abydos' ware is obscure, but very similar jugs have been found in the Early Bronze Age levels at Tel Arad in the south Judaean desert little distant from the Dead Sea. If this proves to be a genuine link it is probably to be connected with the export of Dead Sea pitch to

Ill. 2

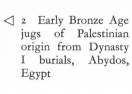

2 Early Bronze Age jugs of Palestinian origin from Dynasty I burials, Abydos, Egypt

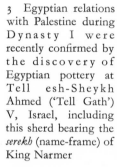

3 Egyptian relations with Palestine during Dynasty I were recently confirmed by the discovery of Egyptian pottery at Tell esh-Sheykh Ahmed ('Tell Gath') V, Israel, including this sherd bearing the *serekh* (name-frame) of King Narmer

Egypt. Two large pottery vessels from Tell Gath in southern Palestine travelled in the opposite direction and carried the incised name of King Narmer, the unifier of Upper and Lower Egypt in Dynasty I.   *Ill. 3*

The political conditions against which these first exchanges were made are unknown. Trade in antiquity very often followed the paths of migration or conquest, and it has been supposed in view of certain parallelisms in the early dynastic civilizations of Sumer and the Nile that they had somehow come into contact. King Narmer himself may have played an important part in exploring the secrets of Asia, for one interpretation of his famous palette in the Cairo Museum sees it as a record of an expedition to Transjordan and a 'taming' of the Twin Rivers. Asiatics certainly appear to be depicted on it, and the panthers with elongated intertwined necks on the reverse of the palette were a current symbol of the Twin   *Ill. 4* Rivers in the Uruk period of predynastic Mesopotamia.

4 The upper side of this palette of Narmer possibly commemorates an expedition to Mesopotamia. Perhaps here, as in Uruk, the felines with elongated intertwined necks symbolize the Twin Rivers, 'tamed' by Narmer. In the lower register, the king (as a bull) gores an Asiatic and destroys a walled town with a central *tell*

Metalworking in Palestine during the Late Chalcolithic and Early Bronze I periods was in the hands of itinerant tinkers (ancestors perhaps of the Biblical Kenites) whose hoards of copper instruments have recently been found at Nahal Mishmar by the Dead Sea and at Kfar Monash on the Haifa–Tel Aviv road. Ores for making these tools and weapons most likely came from Edom (southern Transjordan) or southern Anatolia and whilst the Mishmar hoard is in general far superior to contemporary Egyptian weapons, the Monash hoard contains tools of Egyptian type. Some of the Mishmar objects, especially the copper crowns and maces, are advanced in technique and the *cire perdue* (lost wax) process of casting, still unknown in Egypt, was well advanced in Anatolia by the Early Bronze II period, as instanced by the remarkable copper statuettes from Tell Tainat (Phase G) in the Amuq plain, decorated with hair and ornaments of beaten gold. These examples attest the early achievements of the Syro-Pales-

Ill. 5

5   The important hoard of metalware recently discovered in the Nahal Mishmar cave near the Dead Sea is possibly loot from an Early Bronze Age shrine. It contains crowns, elaborately cast sceptres like this one, vessels and weapons, mostly of copper, and pieces of worked hippopotamus ivory. About 3000 B C

tinian as compared with Egyptian smiths: nor is there anything to equal them in contemporary Mesopotamia. Pieces of silver from Late Chalcolithic Byblos and a complete silver bowl from an Early Bronze I context at Tell Farah near Nablus indicate that their skill was not confined to copper and bronze.

Egyptians were not the only foreigners to show interest in these material resources. Sargon of Akkad (2330–2295 B C), the first Semitic dynast of Mesopotamia, and his grandson Naram-sin claimed dominion 'from the Upper to the Lower Sea', that is from the Mediterranean to the Persian Gulf, and tell in their inscriptions of expeditions to the 'Cedar Forest' and the 'Mountain of Silver'. These localities are almost certainly Mount Lebanon and the Taurus range and indeed the Amanus is expressly mentioned in a text which describes the extent of Naram-sin's rule. But we cannot ascertain the political relationship of these western districts to Mesopotamia in Sargon's day, for the third-millennium civilization of Syria is little known, though archaic cylinder seals show distinct Early Dynastic influence. The recent discovery of Akkadian seals at Ugarit has led to the suggestion that the Akkadians maintained a trading fleet in Syrian waters as a northern parallel to Sargon's trading enterprises with Magan (Oman?) and Meluḫḫa (India?) on the Lower Sea.

Ill. 7

Roughly contemporaneously with the rise of Semitic Akkadian culture in Sumer, Semitic nomads entered the fertile crescent introducing a complex of pottery and other artefacts which characterize the Middle Bronze Age and has initially strong north Mesopotamian leanings.

These 'Western Semites' are known from the beginning of recorded historical references late in the third millennium BC. Later we find two ill-distinguished groups of peoples – Amorites and Canaanites – in possession of the Syro-Palestinian area, the former northerly and easterly, the latter southerly and westerly, but belonging to the same Semitic stock, speaking basically the same language, and differing in little besides name. There were, however, cultural differences, which stem from the fact that the Amorite group ('westerners' as their name, given them by the Sumerians, means) assimilated Sumerian and North Syrian Hurrian elements, whilst the Canaanite 'low-landers' (or perhaps 'purple-dyers') assimilated Mediterranean elements on the coast and became strongly influenced by Egyptian ways of thought and expression.

Of the excavated Amorite cities, Byblos is the first to enter the pages of written history. The city, and the cedars that its inhabitants traded from the slopes of Mt Lebanon, are noted in Egyptian records about 2600 BC when the Pharaoh Sneferu (Dynasty IV) imported forty shiploads of cedar logs for shipbuilding. Well-preserved cedar beams were found propping up his burial chamber entrance in the southern pyramid at Dahshur, and in 1954, beside the Great Pyramid of Giza, the funerary boat of his successor, Kheops, was discovered intact with its cedarwood fittings still retaining, it is said, some of their original odour. Fragments of alabaster vases bearing royal serekhs (the square figures that enclose royal or divine names) found at Byblos are dated even earlier, to Egypt's Dynasty II; it is, therefore, possible that Egypt's contact with Byblos goes back to the dawn of Egyptian history. Byblos is also the earliest city of the western seaboard to be mentioned in Mesopotamian texts. As *Ku-ub-la* it appears in a text from Drehem in the Ur III period (about 2100 BC) when it appears to have been ruled by an Akkadian *patesi* or governor. In the nineteenth century

6 Important for placing Western Asia into the better-known framework of Egyptian chronology, this stone vase fragment excavated at Byblos bears the name of Kha-sekhemwy, a pharaoh of Egypt's Dynasty II (*c.* 2650 BC)

7 Evidence for Mesopotamian cultural domination of North Syria in the later third millennium is best seen at Tell Chuera, but cylinder seals from other sites, such as these from Carchemish and North Syria, show Sumerian designs

the ambitious Shamshi-Adad I of Assyria, the first ruler to create a unified empire in Syria and northern Mesopotamia, claims to have set up stelae on the coast of Lebanon. This enterprise was probably more commercial than political. Shamshi-Adad's control of the Assyrian traders established at Kültepe (Kanesh) in Anatolia, his treaty with Carchemish and overlordship of the caravan city of Mari, all testify to his commercial concerns and the establishment of lively caravan trade.

In Dynasty VI the Egyptian trade with Byblos was on a surer footing and Egyptian texts begin to record special Byblos ships constructed for trade with the port. Whether Byblians or Egyptians manned these ships is not certain, but the recorded facts suggest that Egypt was the prime financier in this trade and led the Mediterranean shipping of the period.

In Byblos herself, evidence from monuments suggests that it was in the strong Dynasty XII (from *c.* 1990 BC)

8, 9 Gifts of the Egyptian pharaohs to princes of Byblos. The obsidian jar (*above*), bound with gold, is exactly similar to jars found in Dynasty XII tombs at Dahshur, Egypt. It is inscribed with the word *tpt*, 'quality oil'; the lid bears the cartouches of Amenemhet (Ammenemes) III. The lid of the gold-embellished obsidian box (*left*), is inlaid with the titles of Amenemhet IV in silver hieroglyphs. Royal Tombs, Byblos, 1840–1790 B C

10–12 A scallop-shaped Egyptian-style jewel (*above*) from a royal tomb at Byblos bears the name 'Ypshemu-abi Prince of Kapna' inserted in bad hieroglyphs in the cartouche – probably by a local jeweller. A square pendant (*Ill. 12* below) inlaid with semi-precious stones copies XII Dynasty work, representing a Horus shrine in which sit two royal figures. Objects of local style include a green paste jug (*Ill. 11* right) with gold bands, part of a treasure probably originating at Byblos

13-15   Golden regalia from the Byblos tombs: a diadem, a Horus-hawk collar and a scimitar-shaped sceptre. The decorations on the diadem are Egyptian in origin: *djed* pillar, symbol of renewed kingship; *waz* sceptre, symbol of well-being; *ankh* sign symbolizing life, and the cobra (uraeus) symbolizing royalty. The sceptre bears the name Ypshemu-abi in inlaid hieroglyphs. The Horus collar, whilst of Egyptian inspiration, shows Canaanite details. Unfortunately for purposes of chronological cross-reference, only one ruler of Byblos is mentioned in XIII Dynasty Egyptian records – Enten or Yantin-Ammu, who ruled *c.* 1740 B C

that relationships with Egypt were especially close. Royal tombs built into the cliffs on the shore of Byblos have been found with their treasures intact, and objects from rifled tombs have found their way to museums in Paris and Beirut. Amongst the intact tombs are those of Abi-shemu (Abi-is-my-father) and his son Ypshemu-abi (my-father's-name-is-good), contemporaries of Pharaohs Amenemhet III and IV (*c.* 1840–1785 B C). An obsidian ointment jar bearing the cartouche of Amenemhet III was found in Abi-shemu's tomb and a gift box of incense from Amenemhet IV in the tomb of his son; whilst to unnamed kings had been sent golden pectorals, other pieces of jewellery and jars of salve.

Ill. 8

Ills. 9, 10, 12

Ills. 13, 14

Although themselves Semites, the kings of Byblos are invested with such Egyptian titles as 'prince', 'count', or 'sheikh of sheikhs'. Their precise political standing in relation to Egypt is unknown, but they were probably vassal kings or high commissioners controlling a local population subject to Egypt. Foreign place-names in lists of Amenemhet III's reign, which covered the second half of the nineteenth century B C, show that the entire coast

22

as far north as the Nahr el-Kebir was included in the
Egyptian political sphere as well as the inland plain of
the Beqa'a. It has been suggested that the gift jars
presented to the Byblian kings might have contained the
very chrism (consecrated oil and balm) of investiture
which the pharaohs of a later period sent to their Syrian
allies, and that the gold-inlaid curved sceptres found in
the tombs are symbols of temporal power from the hand
of Egypt, but evidence for an Egyptian 'Empire' in
Palestine–Syria is insufficient.

Some of the objects found in the royal tombs of Byblos
(*e.g.* tridents with elongated central spike) may be of
Caucasian origin, but the majority naturally show the
influence of Egypt. Alongside this influence, however,
there is a recognizable local style. A golden pectoral, for
instance, depicting the Hathor cow suckling Amenemhet III and a scallop-shaped pendant from the tomb of
Ypshemu-abi might have passed in an Egyptian bazaar,
but any Egyptian jeweller would have noticed innova-
tions and inaccuracies in design. Collars of gold-foil with
a beaten design of the Horus-hawk copy a well-known

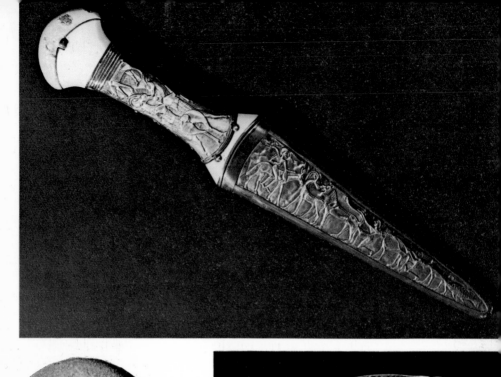

16–20 Deposits buried beneath the temple at
Byblos in the early second millennium BC contained masterpieces of Canaanite-Amorite goldwork. The scabbard sheath of the ivory-handled
dagger (Ill. 16) shows a peasant herding, with
two assistants, the unlikely flock of goat, lion,
baboon, dog and fish. Without Egyptian
influence, the handle-foil (Ill. 17) depicts a noble
in the elongated style (found also in Byblos
statuettes) as well as confronted goats – a
Semitic theme. Granulation and wire-work
were applied to the gold shaft-foils of the
fenestrated ceremonial axe (Ill. 18) and to the
votive inlaid vase (Ill. 19). Ill. 20 a wall-painting
from the tomb of Khnumhotep at Beni Hasan,
depicts nomadic Semites bringing eye-paint to
Egypt c. 1890 BC

Egyptian type, but again the treatment of the feathers and the action of the bird are un-Egyptian, whilst the egg-and-tongue design on the outer border is a device which becomes peculiarly Phoenician in later times and hence passed into the art of Greece.

Ill. 21

Ill. 17

Objects found in the temple, as distinct from the royal tombs, at Byblos are more characteristic of local Amorite craftsmanship. A gold-foil, once the cover of a scabbard, shows a peasant mounted on a donkey herding with the help of two assistants the incongruous flock of a goat, lion, baboon, dog and fish. The features of the peasants are reminiscent of the famous painting in an Egyptian tomb at Beni Hasan, of the family of the Asiatic 'Abisha'

Ill. 20

arriving in Egypt with their goods mounted on donkeys. The men, stubby and black-bearded, have the same bird-like faces with hooked nose. The Beni Hasan painting fills in further details of these semi-nomadic peasants, dressed in long multi-coloured tunics and the clanswomen in gaily patterned dresses (no two alike) and red leather boots. Their weapons are the spear and throwing stock, and their music that of the harp. In the painting we see them bringing eye-paint and two fine desert gazelles for the prince buried here in about the year 1890 BC.

The dagger-handle sheath from Byblos shows even better than the scabbard local Amorite artistic ideas, with the characteristic elongation and the symmetrical position-

Ill. 16

ing of the two goats, whilst objects of greater luxury from the temple show a technical mastery of goldsmithing equal to that of Egypt. Gold-foils from crescentic Syrian

Ill. 18

axes bear granulated designs of religious scenes, whilst a circular pendant and a fine gold vase are not only granu-

Ill. 19

lated but elaborately inlaid with lapis lazuli and other stones. In this vase we have the only surviving example of those elaborate metal vessels borne by the bearded and white-clad Syrian and Lebanese tribute bearers depicted in Egyptian mural paintings of Dynasty XVIII.

21 Obelisks standing in an enclosure behind the temple at Byblos probably embodied divine presences or theophanies. They exemplify an aniconic tendency in Semitic religion which is later expressed in Phoenician baetyl worship

Minoans in Levantine Ports

The merchants of Minoan Crete began to play an important part in this new internationalism opened by Dynasty XII trade. The distinctive light-on-dark pottery of the Middle Minoan II period reached Byblos, Ras Shamra,

22 Very few XII Dynasty objects have been found in Crete. This broken statue from Knossos belonged to User, probably more of a private enterprise merchant than an 'official'

23 Palace frescoes at Mari depict an investiture scene in a double panel (a two-room temple?) set in a garden of symbolic trees and animals. In the upper part of the panel, Zimri-lim receives the sceptre and circlet from Ishtar

N. Cyprus and Qatna on the Orontes as well as reaching Dynasty XII cities such as Kahun, Gurob, Abydos and Harageh in Egypt. It is thus obviously valuable for the archaeologists engaged in the building of a general chronological framework to have found identical Minoan II vessels in Byblos and, for instance, in a Middle Helladic period context at Lerna on the Argolid coast of Greece; or to have ascertained that the Middle Minoan IIa sherds from Lahun belonged to a settlement of workmen engaged in building a pyramid for Senusret II (1895–1877 BC). Similarly, contemporary Egyptian imports to Crete include a Dynasty XII statuette of User found at Knossos and scarabs of the Middle Kingdom from Platanos. Of even greater value than these early second millennium exchanges is the discovery of a little Early Minoan III pottery in graves of the rather isolated Early Bronze Age culture of Cyprus, which had a more local character than any in the Bronze Age Mediterranean. Soon Crete became as accomplished in technology as her eastern neighbours and even surpassed them in the working of many finer materials. The finely worked vessels of rock-crystal,

Ill. 22

obsidian and other difficult stones found in the Minoan palace at Kato Zakro in East Crete show how in later times Minoan craftsmanship surpassed that of contemporary Egypt and provides good reason for the ready markets Minoans found in Levantine ports.

The archaeological evidence for this commercial contact is put in more positive light by the Old Babylonian period cuneiform archives from Mari on the Middle Euphrates. This old Sumerian city, now placed in the centre of Semitic nomadic tribes, was ruled at this period by Amorite dynasts of which Zimri-lim, a contemporary of Babylon's Hammurabi, was the most important. There is frequent mention in the documents of his reign of trade with Byblos (especially garments from *Gubla*) and Ugarit, and quite clearly copper was reaching Mari from Cyprus. But even beyond, *Kaptaru* (Biblical Caphtor, Crete) is the source of fine objects such as the caphtorite juglet presented by Zimri-lim to the king of Razama. A 'caphtorite' sword is also listed in an inventory; its pommel and base are bound with gold and its top is inlaid with lapis lazuli.

These early contacts with the older civilization of Mesopotamia had important consequences for Minoan Crete. The royal palace of Zimri-lim of Mari, which the Minoans visited, is one of the most important surviving buildings of the ancient world. Complicated in plan and advanced in structure – it incorporated the brick arch – with its open internal courtyards, storerooms, toilet rooms and with excellent drainage and plumbing, it probably formed the pattern for the Minoan palaces. The

Ill. 23

Mari palace frescoes depicting religious scenes and the local Amorite population painted on stucco antedate the frescoes of Hagia Triada and other Cretan palaces and it was probably from these and the fragmentary frescoes from contemporary Alalakh that Minoan wall-paintings were derived. Under Zimri-lim, Mari rose to prosperity as a caravan city; her business archives speak of links through Babylon with the traders of the Persian Gulf ports, and Elam and Sippar appear to have maintained private links, providing tin and other materials in exchange for the timber oil and wine of Syria.

It was partly the silver ores of the Taurus mountains that attracted the Minoans to North Syria. Silver was still a rare metal in Egypt in Dynasty XII times and indeed was never plentiful there. The only substantial discovery of silverwork in Egypt is a hoard of cups, many of them purposely crushed and folded, found in a votive deposit in the temple at Tôd, twenty miles south of Luxor. They had been buried in four copper boxes bearing the cartouches of Amenemhet II (1927–1893 BC). The cups are very similar in both shape and decoration to later Minoan metalware, but their early date and the few lumps of lapis lazuli and cuneiform seals found with them suggest an origin in some North Syrian coastal city in which Minoan silversmiths learned their craft. The same may be said of

Ill. 24

two delicately fluted silver teapots from the royal tombs at Byblos, which are more Syrian in shape.

24 Objects of Minoan affinities have been found in the royal tombs of Byblos, but this silver-fluted 'teapot' from the tomb of Abishemu is Syrian rather than Cretan. The Tôd treasure from Egypt and a group of golden disks with spiral designs recently found on the Syrian coast suggest that local workshops operated in the second millennium, perhaps with Aegean participation

Very little is at present known of the other coastal cities, such as Tyre and Sidon, in the early part of the second millennium, or, as also in the case of Byblos, with their relations, political and ethnical, with the inhabitants of the Lebanese mountains. A remarkable series of copper statuettes found mainly on both slopes of the Lebanon range and dated by a few associated objects to the Middle Bronze Age (c. 1700 BC) tell us something of the physical type of the people dwelling in the mountains. They were short and stocky, wide of eye and pronounced of chin. Their trim beards, and swept-back plaited hair, are found on contemporary work in Mari and in later times in the Hurrian town of Tell Halaf in northern Syria. The racial type portrayed in the Lebanese statuettes is pronouncedly North Syrian, and indeed related statuettes occur in the Turkish Hatay and farther into Anatolia. The male statuettes are dressed in a manner eminently suitable to mountain herdsmen, with a short kilt fitted with a broad brace or belt, probably of leather laced in front with a tasselled cord.

It can be concluded from material found in tombs at Lebea, Kafer-Djarra and elsewhere that besides settling in the coastal cities, attested at Byblos and Sidon, the Middle Bronze Age population, archaeologically characterized by pottery including elegant 'button-based' jars, extended a considerable distance into the hills. It is probable that in the immediate Lebanon area the Canaanite population was limited to the fertile coastal strip and, as recent excavations have shown, to the plain of the Beqa'a, leaving the older population stratum of the hills unmolested or employing them perhaps as porters of goods to Palestine beyond whose population at this period, although given the archaeologically unsatisfactory name of 'Canaanite', was probably predominantly of the more northerly Amorite stock.

The royal archives of Mari show that in the early part of the second millennium BC the Amorites were essentially nomadic in their way of life. One of the loosely affiliated Semitic tribes in the Mari region bore the name Habiru, a name used in many parts of the Near East at this period to denote that status of tribes without legal affiliations to any particular kingdom. Now although there is insufficient philological evidence directly to connect this name with that of the later Hebrews, accounts in the Mari archives, and in the legal tablets from Nuzi in north-east Mesopotamia relating to Hurrian and Habiru people, introduce us to political and legal habits with which the patriarchal history of the Bible makes us familiar. It is probable that it was from some such tribe that Abraham's 'wandering Aramaean' father came. It was as the husband of the daughter of a sheikh of such a tribe that the homesick Egyptian traveller Sinuhe found himself in the twentieth century BC. In his account of his adventures he describes vividly the Bedouin life and the country: 'Figs there were in it and grapes. It had more wine than water. Plentiful its honey, abundant its olives. Its trees bore every fruit. Barley was there and wheat. There was no limit to the kind of cattle.' Even so, Sinuhe could not bear to stay, die and be buried, 'with but a sheepskin for a shroud', in a strange land, and gave up the sand 'to them who are in it'.

The Hyksos

From other details of Sinuhe's story it appears that Asiatic nomadic tribes were already beginning to make incursions into Egypt soon after 2000 BC. After the Middle Kingdom, by about 1750 BC, the Hyksos, a group of nomad herdsmen kings, swept over Syria and Palestine and imposed a foreign Dynasty on Egypt. It is possible that in the southern aspect of this mass folk-movement the conquering element was Canaanite or Amorite. Some of the earliest Hyksos bore Canaanite names and the deities whose worship was introduced to Egypt by the Hyksos kings were largely Canaanite ones. The weight of the Hyksos incursion came, however, from the more northerly Hurrian region and waves of Hurrian settlers appear to have introduced Hurrian place-names to Palestine. They brought superiority in metallurgy and weapons and, above all, the use of the horse, domesticated beyond the Caspian by Indo-European peoples, and the horse-drawn chariot as a new and unassailable weapon of war. Important city sites from Palestine to Egypt were reconstructed under the Hyksos with rampart and glacis for fortifications as a countermeasure to the battering-ram and are a clear indication of a widespread and organized type of warfare introduced in the world of the Middle Bronze Age.

The Hyksos migration ushers in a century of obscurity in the history of the Levant. Presumably the old Canaanite aristocracy of merchants and business men was now replaced by alien feudal chariot knights installed as a ruling class over the native population. But even now, Egypt cannot have been isolated from channels of trade, for objects bearing the name of the Hyksos king, Khian, *Ill. 25* found their way to Knossos, Iraq and the Hittite capital at Boghazköy. The black juglets with white-filled dot design known often as 'Hyksos juglets' appear in Egypt at the end of the Dynasty XII at Kahun, Lisht, and

25 The Hyksos king Khian, though ruling Egypt during an obscure period, the Second Intermediate Period, fostered overseas relations. This alabastron lid from Knossos bears his name, as does a jar fragment from the Hittite capital, Boghazköy

particularly at Tell el-Yahudîyeh, from which they take their name. The currency of these jugs, in Middle Bronze II, whilst they cannot be regarded as specifically 'Hyksos' and rather perhaps originated in the Lebanon, shows extensive intercourse between Egypt, Palestine and Syria, becoming more pronounced in the case of the latter countries in Middle Bronze IIc.

When Egyptian records recommence we find besides the establishment of the Hyksos in Palestine, a new Indo-European knighthood in North Syria, that of the Mitannians dominating from their capital, Waššugani, possibly Tell Fecheriyeh, on the Upper Ḥabur River, the peoples of that territory and the northern seaboard. It was a southward movement first of the Hurrians, and later their Indo-Aryanized Mitannian overlords from the Upper Ḥabur region into the North Syrian desert, which probably pushed the Hyksos groups into Egypt, and later crystalized opposition to Egyptian Syria.

CHAPTER TWO

The Egyptian Domination
of the Levant

It was Ahmosis I, founder of Dynasty XVIII, who in 1570 BC crushed the Hyksos Dynasty, which since the late eighteenth century had been maintained by superiority of arms in the capital of Avaris in the Nile Delta. During this period the Hyksos appear to have retrenched themselves in their strongly fortified Palestinian towns and the so-called Hyksos scarabs with their delicate spiral designs are found on all sites between Syria and the Nile, associated often in coastal sites with the Tell el-Yahudîyeh ware. Besides scarabs, horse-bits occasionally appear in Middle Bronze IIc contexts. At Gaza at South Palestine the unique phenomenon of the burial of soldiers with their horses, a custom of Indo-Aryan origin, has been found during excavation.

Ill. 26

The Asiatic campaigns of Ahmosis are little known, although, towards 1525 apparently, Tuthmosis I continued them as far as the Euphrates. It was Tuthmosis III, of whose campaigns we are graphically informed by the reliefs carved on the walls of the temple at Karnak, who finally came to grips with the Canaanites and Hurrians in their homelands (1483–1463 BC). Under the threat of these

Ills. 27, 28

26 Bronze 'Hyksos' bit from Tell el-Ajjul (Gaza). Sixteenth century BC

27, 28 Tuthmosis III (1504–1450) by many victories and much conquest firmly established the Egyptian Empire. He is seen here (*left*), vanquishing Asiatics on the seventh pylon in the temple complex at Karnak. The names of subjugated cities are shown below him. Opposite is a view of his Festival Hall, not far from the pylon, a temple unique in Egyptian architecture that is modelled on the type of campaign tent used by the pharaoh in Syria

campaigns the defences of the Palestinian farming towns were greatly strengthened. With three hundred princes and their *mar-janni* (charioteer knights) shut up within her, Megiddo stood siege for seven months. The presence of these charioteer knights in the plain of Sharon provides clear indication of the dominance of Hurrian elements in Palestine at this period.

A key-point in the fifth Syrian campaign of Tuthmosis III was the capture of the northern Canaanite inland city of Arwad (Aradus, situated in a strategic position probably opposite Arwad island), which features now for the first time as a city of great wealth. Along with Arwad the pharaoh gained possession of the Syrian coast towns of Simyra and Ullaza and a stretch of the north Lebanese-south Syrian coast called Djahi in Egyptian texts. Obviously it was harvest-time; the large booty exacted by Tuthmosis, and recorded in the triumphal narrative at Karnak, included the grain being ground on the threshing floors as well as horses, silver dishes, lead, copper, lapis lazuli (not a local product), green feldspar (a crystalline mineral), incense, oil, jars of honey, and 6428 jars of wine.

'Behold', says the official communiqué, 'the army of His Majesty was drunk.'

The precise nature of what Tuthmosis and his successor Amenophis II hoped to achieve by these campaigns is doubtful, but it can be surmised that the accounts of these campaigns written on the walls of the temple at Karnak are somewhat exaggerated and that the elaborate 'booty' must on occasions have been gifts from these prosperous commercial towns to avert the costly catering for an un-welcome Egyptian visit. Kadesh on the Orontes, the fountainhead of 'Hyksos' disturbance, was however com-pletely destroyed, and the prestige of Egypt was felt in this area until the decline of the New Kingdom.

Despite the ravaging of the Mitanni lands, the destruc-tion of the Mitannian army was not achieved. But such was the lack of unity between the southern city-states and the great northern powers, and the impact of the friendly overtures made by the prince of Alašia and the great king of Ḥatti to the pharaoh, that the rebellious Hurrian in the North Syrian plains evidently acquiesced in the establish-ment of an Egyptian protectorate over Syria and Canaan.

Each city-state in these regions maintained independent relationships with Egypt, giving rise to a complicated diplomacy. In the Canaanite cities some sort of supervisory Egyptian government was set up, and mobile sea-borne squadrons of Egyptian soldiers were at readiness to maintain peace.

This subjection imposed on Canaan conditions unlikely to foster the development of national enterprise in any direction except that of trade; but the Mitannian alliance, now with its western bastion at Alalakh in the Orontes valley, held more of its own. Its relations with Egypt were cemented by dynastic marriages between the royal families. The mother of Amenophis III (about 1401–1362 BC) was a Mitannian princess. His son, Amenophis IV, also included amongst his royal brides a daughter of the Mitannian king Tušratta, well known from Egyptian records of this period.

The Mitannians

Very little is yet known of the artistic, religious and other cultural traditions of the Hurrians and Mitanni. The domination of these latter was very variable in extent; the heart of their kingdom was known to the Egyptians as Naharina, the 'river land' around the courses of the Ḥabur and Baliḫ. But, outside this, they appear to have established in late Hyksos times, probably as part of a Hurrian social pattern, a ruling knighthood in the Syrian and northern Palestinian cities. This appears to have been Indo-Aryan; not only do many Mitanni rulers bear Indo-Aryan names but they also worshipped Indra, Varuna and

29 The Mitannian king in rounded head-dress and rolled-border mantle stands before his goddess. Between them is the *ankh*, sign of life. Cylinder seal design

30–32 A cylinder seal of the Mitannian period from Tripoli shows Cretan influence; two youths, with the typically Minoan narrow waists and flowing hair, attack a lion. The Mitannian kings standing on each side of a 'sun pillar' in *Ill. 31* above, are perhaps swearing a covenant. A goddess and a bull-man slay a lion on the seal *Ill. 32* right. Note the goddess' fantastic version of the Egyptian crown

other deities of the *Rigveda,* besides employing a system of counting related to Sanskrit. Their adoption on cylinder seals of the 'ankh' (breath of life) symbol and the winged disk of the sun from Egyptian sources suggests the currency among the aristocracy of religious concepts other than those current in Canaan. Perhaps even the chariot racing and lion hunting, those first sports of kings, to which they were addicted, had a religious symbolical meaning which enhanced their popularity as a sport. Mythological subjects on Mitannian seals are largely derived from the Babylonian repertoire, but ritual or symbolical scenes abound and a particular fondness is shown for the sacred tree and heraldically placed animals. Some of these symbolical seals with ox-heads and griffins show some influence of Cretan art-forms, as indeed do those of Kassite Babylonia. Certain seals from the North Syrian coast show direct Cretan borrowings and attest the continuance of relationships as late as the fourteenth century.

Ill. 29

Ills. 30, 31

Ill. 32

33, 34 A bronze statuette found in Egypt depicts a Mitannian prince wearing the Egyptian 'white crown'. He was possibly the bridegroom of an Egyptian princess or sent *au pair*. The white magnesite statue of King Idrimi of Alalakh (*right*), carries a biographical inscription describing his struggles in gaining his throne. Fifteenth century B C

35 During the XVIII Dynasty it was conventional to depict the pharaoh in victorious postures over the traditional enemies of Egypt. Even though Tut-ankh-amun's hold on Asia was weak, he is depicted on this painted wooden box from his tomb 'trampling down hundreds and thousands' of garishly clad Syrians

36, 37 The above reconstruction of merchants of coastal Canaan arriving at an Egyptian port is based on a wall-painting from the tomb of Kenamun at Thebes (*below*). Some of the bartering appears to be done at dock-side souvenir shops, and the bulk cargo of slaves and wine passes into the hands of Kenamun's clerks

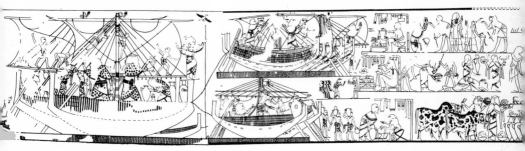

A certain pottery fabric known as Nuzi ware (from its initial discovery at Nuzi or Yorghan Tepe in East Iraq) appears to have been somehow connected with Mitannian expansion and has been found distributed from Boghaz-köy to Nuzi in the east. The light-on-dark-painted designs of water birds, guilloche, daisies and other motifs are derived from local folk art but at Alalakh the painting is greatly influenced by Minoan design and includes lotus and papyrus stems. The chalice-shaped vases with narrow feet surpass in proportion and refinement any created up to that time in the Oriental world.

Ill. 33

The statue of an important Mitannian vassal, King Idrimi (fifteenth century BC) from Alalakh, and a few copper statuettes as well as seal representations illustrate Mitannian kings of the middle second millennium clad in a tall 'mitre' and wearing the thickly bordered mantle peculiar to the Hurrian-Mitannian area. A particularly

Ill. 34

fine statuette from Egypt shows a Mitannian prince, perhaps a member of the Pharaoh's court, affecting the Egyptian crown.

Trade

In Egyptian wall-paintings of about this time the purple-robed Canaanites of the Lebanese coast appear bringing their merchandise. The purple dye, for which the Phoenician coast became famous in later times, is first named in a cuneiform text from Ras Shamra (Ugarit), showing that a certain quantity of raw wool had been delivered amongst weavers who were responsible for the distribution of the dyed cloth. Although the shell-fish (*murex*) from which the dye could be made has a wide distribution in the Mediterranean it is in the region of Tyre and Sidon that the best varieties occur.

In Dynasty XVIII (1570–1314 BC) we have our first reference to the native shipping which carried these wares to the Delta. Such ships, in no way comparable with the large vessels built at the command of Queen Hatshepsut

Ill. 37

in about 1500 BC, could be seen in a wall-painting (now destroyed) from a Theban tomb. The form of the vessel, though basically Egyptian, has a high vertical prow and stern, and sides which appear to be made of wicker. A large paddle acts as a rudder. It is not now the cedar wood which is the chief item of commerce, but wine jars, cloths,

38　Egyptian paintings show tribute horses and chariots of a design similar to this example from the tomb of Amenophis III. The four-spoke wheel was superseded in the Levant in the fourteenth century by a six-spoke variety (*cf. Ills. 35, 49*)

flasks of oil and cattle. Buyers weigh the wares and a good deal of bartering and sampling animates the scene. The wine jars, the circular flasks, and the tall-necked jugs are all recognizably Canaanite, and the bulls of the humped variety native to Syria. Of the merchants themselves, some wear the purple-patterned garments of the coastal cities, others the simpler white Syrian dress, whilst the women are dressed in a frilled white frock and wear their hair loose. Arriving in full sail with the hold so full that a temporary deck can be lashed across it, the ships are soon unloaded by kilted slaves and the sails furled by a host of clambering boys. Other Syrians featured in the wall-paintings, some from Mitannian centres in the Orontes valley. Amongst other articles, they traded ready-made chariots of a lightly framed type similar to that surviving in the tomb of Amenophis III, now in Florence. Egyptian accounts leave no doubt that the ash, hornbeam and willow woods needed for chariot construction were all native to the Mitannian hill lands.

Colonies of Canaanite and Syrian traders were certainly settled in Egypt from the reign of Amenophis II

Ill. 36

Ill. 38

39   Illustrating the international style of Levantine art in the fourteenth century BC, this conical rhyton of coloured faience from a Cypro-Mycenaean grave in Citium is Aegean in shape, but the animal gallop and bull-hunting theme – here Egyptian in flavour – are equally at home in Egypt and Aegean. The red and yellow glazes are overlaid on a ground of bright blue faience

40   Special containers for exports. The red 'spindle bottle' is of a fifteenth-century BC Syrian type and the small black (opium?) flask of about the same date is Cypriot. The oil horn from Kurneh, Egypt, has a dove-head stopper and an ivory base-plate inlaid with a Syrian star

41, 42 Keftians (Cretans?) bring both Syrian and Aegean vessels as tribute to Egypt in this wall-painting from the tomb of Senmut at Thebes. The bucranium decoration on the Mycenaean-type columnar-handled cup is reminiscent of that on an Enkomi cup. *Below*, Syrians in a wall-painting from Sobekhotep's tomb, Thebes (time of Tuthmosis IV) bring gold vessels of artificial flowers, a griffin rhyton and an oil horn (*cf. Ill. 40*)

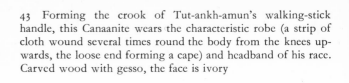

(1440–1415 BC). In his tomb, inscribed sherds of pottery recording the names of foreigners, and objects of foreign design were found. Consequently it was during his reign that the worship of Canaanite deities grew in Egypt and trade on a large scale between Egypt and Syria was opened up. This perhaps explains the appearance in Dynasty XVIII Egypt of Syrianizing elements in Egyptian decoration. In the magnificent tomb of Tut-ankh-amun they become in fact dominating. The themes are not initially predominantly Aegean. The motif of rams feeding at a stylized sacred tree is probably of Mesopotamian or North Syrian origin transmitted by Canaanites.

Ills. 35, 43

Ras Shamra (Ugarit)

Although Byblos still continued as an important port in the mid-second millennium, Ras Shamra ('Fennel-head' in Arabic) situated on a coastal bluff between Iskenderun and Latakia cornered the foreign markets. The ancient name of the port was Ugarit, a name already known before its archaeological discovery in the 1920s from Hittite documents and the so-called Tell el-Amarna Letters, an archive of cuneiform tables containing the correspondence of princes of Syria and Palestine with Amenophis III and IV and discovered in Upper Egypt. Ugarit was probably the first great international port in history. Her cosmopolitan urbanity, diplomacy, suavity and adaptability anticipate the character of modern Levantine life, and her mixed cultural status must have been something like that of present-day Beirut.

Many of the buildings and objects found at Ugarit agree considerably with the cultural status of other cities in North Syria in the second millennium, but its importance in the history of Levantine civilization is that

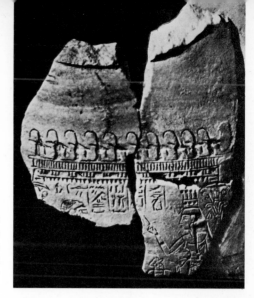

44, 45 Two wedding commemorations from Ras Shamra. The scarab celebrates the union of Amenophis III and Queen Tiy; the alabaster vase shows Niqmadu of Ugarit with an Egyptian princess and must commemorate his marriage or accession

western influence is unparalleled at any other site. During the period 1800–1600 B C Minoan pottery was being imported as in other Syrian towns; but nowhere as in Ugarit did Aegeans form a trading colony with separate living quarters in the harbour and in the 'ghetto' of the town. Beneath their stately homes in the harbour region they buried their dead in chambered tombs of careful construction under the house floors. After 200 years of service these chambers became filled to capacity with bones and pottery, and thus no attempt could be made to preserve the careful burial rites of their Aegean homelands.

The political history of Ugarit reconstructed from the archives found in the city begins early in the fourteenth century with the reign of Ammishtamru I, a vassal of Egypt and author of at least one of the Amarna letters. During his reign and that of his son Niqmadu, inscribed vases and scarabs of Amenophis III and Amenophis IV *Ill. 44* reached Ugarit, and Niqmadu himself, as appears from a painted 'marriage vase', married an Egyptian princess. *Ill. 45*

After relations between Ugarit and Minoan Crete had some time been broken, the Mycenaeans appear to have founded a substantial trading colony and must have formed an influential element in the Ugaritic population

46–48 Among the tribute brought by Keftians painted in the tomb of Rekhmire at Thebes are a conical rhyton (cf. Ill. 39) and ingots like Ill. 67. Ills. 47, 48 are ingots of later Cypriot origin recovered in 1960 from a shipwreck of about 1200 BC off Cape Gelidonya, southern Turkey

49 Ivory game box and mirror handles from Enkomi, c. 1180 BC. The bull-hunt is reminiscent of the Ras Shamra gold bowl (cf. Ill. 62). The warrior-and-griffin combat on the mirror handles is Oriental but with Mycenaean traits

during the city's most flourishing period from 1400 to 1200 BC. The tombs in the port area (Minet el-Beida) were fully used and quantities of Mycenaean pots were found in them.

One of the outstanding results of recent excavations has been to show the deep penetration of Mycenaean trade into the Levant. Merchants from the Greek mainland, perhaps along with Cretans, first established contact with Egypt during the Amarna period when artistic relationships between Egypt and the Aegean were marked. As regards Syria, in the Middle Minoan III and Late Minoan I periods imports of Cretan pottery became rare, and the remaining centuries of the second millennium BC saw an ever-increasing volume of Mycenaean trade and influence. It is difficult to know how far we can speak of Mycenaean *colonization* in the Levant. The Ras Shamra evidence certainly implies it and at Sarepta near Beirut a complete Mycenaean tomb was found. But colonies at Tell Sukas and Al Mina remain theoretical. There is, however, a distinct possibility of a Mycenaean settlement at Tarsus and with the colonization of Rhodes and the recent evidence for settlement in Caria it is possible that the Mycenaeans aimed to plant a chain of colonies extending to Syria. A key factor was the relationship with Cyprus. It is strange in view of its proximity and great mineral wealth that the Minoans showed little interest in the island. Trade relations were on a very small scale, and had ceased altogether during the period 1600–1400 BC.

Ill. 41

It seems that the first sustained contact between Cyprus and the Aegean was made by the importation of pottery from the Greek mainland by the eastern Cypriot cities, particularly Enkomi, Milea, Maroni and Hala Sultan Tekke, as well as nearby Greek Citium. This is pottery of the Mycenaean IIIa period (1400–1300 BC). By the subsequent IIIb period (1300–1230 BC) the Cypriot potters were producing their own version of Mycenaean pottery

49

called 'Levanto-Helladic' or 'Cypro-Mycenaean' ware, painted with highly attractive designs and most amusing of all Mycenaean vase painting; their liveliness and originality was characteristic of Cyprus in the ancient world.

Probably as a result of Mycenaean trade the port towns of Cyprus grew to wealth and both imported Mycenaean IIIb wares and local Levanto-Helladic are well represented. With both Rhodes and Cyprus acting as entrepôts for Mycenaean goods, and the activity of importers in Alalakh, Ugarit, Gaza and elsewhere, IIIb pottery reached inland sites in Palestine and Syria. In the two Biblical sites of Lachish and Hazor in Galilee it was found beneath the burnt strata attributed to the Hebrew conquest. At the same time the local Cypriot non-Mycenaean ceramics such as the delicate milk-bowl ware reached Palestine and Syria in quantity, suggesting that Cypriots were extremely active in the pottery trade at this period and indicating the important cultural status of the island in Mycenaean times. The evidence suggests that Mycenaean potters chose the island as a distribution centre for their wares and that IIIb pottery and Cypro-Mycenaean ware was locally produced on the island.

CHAPTER THREE

The Period of Hittite and Philistine Domination

Hittite power in south-east Anatolia reached its zenith under Suppiluliumas (1380–1355 BC). It was he who attacked and conquered the Mitannians, and the firm foothold he gained over North Syria brought him face to face with the Egyptian power. The Ugaritic king Niqmadu paid tribute to him in the fourteenth century, and throughout the thirteenth century the dynasty of Ugarit was subservient to the Hittites. The palace archives reveal the intervention of the 'great kings' and 'great queens' of the Hittites in the affairs of the city, though she retained independence in her commercial affairs. Thus Ugarit had passed from the world of Amarna into the orbit of the Hittites, whose expansion in the latter half of the fourteenth century BC extended to Kadesh and incorporated Halab (Aleppo), Mukish and other small North Syrian states which finally fell under the domination of the important Hittite city of Carchemish on the Euphrates. Rich in economic resources, but poor in military strength and constantly menaced by the Amorite state of Amurru in the hinterland, Ugarit – and doubtless other cities whose detailed history is lost – were torn between Egyptian and Hittite policies until Amenophis IV's weakness gave way to Hittite interest in Syria as the Amarna letters record.

The important cuneiform texts discovered in the royal library at Ugarit tell us something of the city's western policies. Naturally relations with Cyprus were strong, and here trade relations had a partly political basis. The palace archives unveil for us a political episode linking the city with Cyprus. Two princes of Ugarit, Hishmi-Sharruma and Arad-Sharruma, because of a fault committed against King Ammishtamru II, a close relation, merited banishment to the land of Alašia. Tablets recording this judgement were made out by the Dowager Queen Ahatmilku in the presence of Hittite and Mitannian royalty. To such dynastic history may be added the official request for the presence of Egyptian workmen in Ugarit made by Niqmadu II. Amongst documents found in recent excavations at Ugarit is a letter from a southern Anatolian city requesting relief supplies of grain as well as a letter from the king of Alašia mentioning the dangers of famine. All provide evidence of the continued wealth and influence of the port.

The numerous business documents found at Ras Shamra show that the Mycenaeans were not the only merchants to form a colony. Ashdodites (*adddy*) Egyptians (*mṣry*), Canaanites (*kn'ny*) – for the inhabitants of Ugarit did not regard themselves as strictly Canaanite – are mentioned as well as an important colony of merchants from Ura in Cilicia, who acted as a diplomatic corps and as 'merchants of the Sun' (*i.e.* the Hittite king) when Ugarit fell into the Hittite commercial network. Because of the close link that existed in the world of the late second millennium between commercial and political activity, overseas transactions were conducted in no haphazard way. By virtue of their quasi-diplomatic status, the merchant colonists were placed under the control of a prefect who saw to it that despite their privileges they were not allowed to acquire real estate in the city or indeed to reside in it all year round.

50   Clay tablet with Cypro-Minoan-like script from Ras Shamra. Though undeciphered, it confirms Cypriot trade in the city and possibly suggests the use of a Cypro-Minoan script-type peculiar to Ugarit

The presence of Cypriot merchants at Ugarit is attested not only by pottery but by the discovery of clay tablets written in a syllabic script called Cypro-Minoan, which appears to have been brought into use at·Enkomi in the fifteenth century. So far, this script has been found only at Enkomi and Ras Shamra, and despite its name has no recognizable relationship, either with the Cretan Linear A Script or the Linear B Script of Knossos and mainland Mycenaean Greece. Decipherment has made little progress; but it is clear that it was more widely employed within Cypriot trading circles than the paucity of clay tablets suggests, since its signs were used as potters' marks on the Cypro-Mycenaean wares at Ras Shamra and written on a bowl and other small objects.

Ill. 50

For the most part, the return cargoes taken by the Mycenaean ships consisted of perishable raw materials, especially the raw metal from Cyprus, but Aegean acquaintance with the exotic products of the Orient had already begun. Wine jars of a type found stacked in scores in the storerooms of Ugarit have been found in Mycenaean tombs at Argos, Menidi and Athens, similar to jars in which a light wine made of North Syrian grapes was shipped down the coast of Palestine to Egypt. Export from Ugarit of vegetable oils and essences is also mentioned in the texts, but it is not possible to identify them. Spices identified in Mycenaean Linear B tablets from Pylos, Mycenae and Knossos can only have reached the Aegean from some such port as Ugarit: *po-ni-ki-jo* and *ku-pi-ri-jo* are taken to indicate 'Phoenician' and 'Cypriot' spices, whilst sesame (*sa-sa-ma*) and cardamom (*ka-da-mi-no*)

must have come by an overland trade route from Mesopotamia or India to a Levantine port. A few souvenirs
were brought back on these trips, such as the ivory duck-
head finial in an Asine tomb. It was perhaps the children
of an Oriental merchant family of about 1220 BC who
were buried in a cremation tomb at Perati in Attica. Their
tomb contained a haematite cylinder seal of North Syrian
design, an Oriental knife, a steatite cartouche of Ramesses
II and a short Cypro-Minoan inscription. But it was above
all with Thebes in Boeotia that Greek legend preserved
the memory of Oriental contacts. Cadmus, king of that
city, is supposed to have come from Phoenicia in search
of his daughter Europa and to have settled at Thebes in
response to the Delphic oracle. He is said to have brought
with him the art of writing the Semitic alphabetic letters
which became the Greek alphabet. Whilst we have no
proof of this, recent excavations in Mycenaean Thebes
have revealed strong Oriental contacts in ivory work and
other arts. In part of the palace destroyed in Mycenaean
IIIb times were found quantities of Oriental cylinder seals
of the highest quality, some with cuneiform inscriptions

Ill.51

51 Oriental bric-a-brac from a Mycenaean tomb, Perati (Attica), including a Syrian cylinder seal, and a cartouche of Ramesses II

52 Surviving evidence of the perishable goods which spread Near Eastern artistic influence abroad is rare. This carved wooden 'head-cup' from an Egyptian tomb is Syrian, probably Mitannian in origin. Similar cups in blue faience were found at Enkomi, Ras Shamra, Ashur and other sites

assigning them to the Kassite-Babylonian dynasty of the fourteenth century B C, but also including fine examples of Syro-Hittite glyptic. Their discovery gives strong support to the possibility of a kernel of truth in the Cadmean legend.

Canaanite Arts and Crafts

It was in this period of Aegean influence at Ugarit in the fourteenth–thirteenth centuries that the famous epics recording the exploits of the Canaanite gods were committed to writing. It is significant that Kothar, the Ugaritic god of craftsmanship who serves the other gods as architect, hails from Crete. It is thus no wonder that Aegean architects exerted an influence at Ras Shamra.

One of the products that illustrates the keenness of Ugaritic adaptability and helps us to trade her trade is pale blue faience, an Egyptian invention copied at Ugarit and Enkomi. At this latter site Mycenaean stirrup vases and an Egyptian duck-shaped toilet bowl are copied in this material, and faience goblets in the form of the heads of curly haired women wearing black hats of a type found

Ill. 52

53, 54 On the Megiddo ivory (*left*), the Egyptian god Bes has been given wings by the Canaanite artist. The ivory lid from Ras Shamra (*right*), is Mycenaean, though the theme would be well understood in the Levant

at Ras Shamra also occur at Ashur, Mari, Ur and Tell Abu Hawam, the forerunner of the modern port of Haifa.

It is indeed possible that the craftsmen who traded these faience vessels were Mitannians and that some of them were produced in a North Syrian centre, for Mitannian cylinder seals of faience became widespread. Vessels in the form of animal and human heads were popular amongst the Hurrians, and it is likely that the woman-head cups were used in the cult of the Hurrian fertility goddess, Kubaba. Production of multi-coloured faience became the speciality of this Syro-Canaanite group; identical spouted basins coated inside with a brilliant yellow glaze and on the outside with blue-green have been found at Enkomi, Ashur and Tell Fecheriyeh (possibly the site of the Mitannian capital), whilst the superb conical rhyton from Citium in Cyprus is one of the finest faience pieces ever produced. Its design is typical of the mixed Mycenaean-Canaanite style of the Amarna period, and besides its typical Mycenaean shape and decorative elements depicts a (divine?) hunter in Syrian helmet attacking

Ill. 39

55, 56 The beast on the ivory plaque (*right*), compares closely with griffins on Mycenaean ivories. A king and his consort in royal Canaanite dress are engraved on the ivory scabbard sheath (*below*). From Megiddo. Thirteenth to twelfth centuries BC

a herd of bulls. A not dissimilar figure was found on faience fragments from the 'House of Shields' at Mycenae along with faience cups of probable Syrian origin.

Ivory Carvings

A number of interesting ivories have been found in Syria and Palestine, notably at Megiddo and Ugarit, which show affinities with both Mycenaean and Aegean styles (thirteenth century BC). It is, however, often difficult to decide whether they signify the influence of Mycenae on Canaan or vice versa. Motifs such as the 'sacral ivy' on the Megiddo plaques are Mycenaean, but others, like the drooping palm on a box from Tell Fara (Beth Pelet), are Canaanite. The one distinctive beast in the animal repertoire, the winged and plumed griffin, which was enthusiastically adopted by Egyptian art of these centuries, can be shown to have a slight Canaanite antecedence.

Ill. 54

Ill. 55

Other ivories from the Syro-Palestinian area are of a straightforward Egyptianizing type. Quite elaborate scenes were borrowed from Egypt, as those on the Tell

57–60 A major source of Levantine wealth was ivory work. Exported raw ivory tusks have been found at Mycenae, and a carved tusk appears to be the product of a Levantine workshop. In the royal palace of Ugarit, ivory was sumptuously used. The bed-head panels (*Ills. 57, 59*) portray the raising of offspring to the royal house. The two outer panels of *Ill. 57* show the queen praying before the naked fertility goddess. Particularly interesting is the second panel

Ill. 53
Ill. 56

Fara casket showing swamp and banquet scenes, and in addition to these distinctive themes, items of furniture and dress are also Egyptian. Slightly more Canaanite in detail is an ivory scabbard-plaque from Megiddo showing a knight leading naked prisoners before an enthroned king. The layout of the scene is Egyptian, but the throne and garments Canaanite, whilst a general vivacity about the scene and a humorous touch added by the birds picking up the crumbs by the royal throne show a typically Canaanite addition to a set pattern.

In contrast to such genre scenes are motifs on the bedstead fittings in the palace at Ras Shamra. Here we find repeated the official royal Egyptian themes of smiting a kneeling enemy. The delicate modelling undoubtedly owes something to the graceful relief style of the time of Amenophis III. Yet here the Canaanite craftsman has drawn some garments in a local style. The most interesting panel from the bed shows the goddess Hathor facing frontally and feeding two youths at her breast. Not only in this plaque are details wrongly Egyptian one showing the unique relationship of a prince with his goddess. Between the horns of the goddess appears the Hittite royal emblem, a hint of the growing influence of this northern power upon the Ugaritic royal family.

from the right in *Ill. 59* in which the king and pregnant queen – in Canaanite dress – embrace. The third panel suggests that two sons were born and suckled by the mother-goddess Asherah. An ivory oliphant (*Ill. 58*) shows the fertility goddess Ashtart between sphinxes. Carving in the round is illustrated by the small head of a Canaanite queen (*Ill. 60* below). Her eyes were inlaid and her hair-locks added in gold. Late fourteenth to early thirteenth centuries B C

Hittite influence counted for little in artistic circles in Canaan and few of the ivories show anything of the heavy Hittite style. Specimens of beaten metalwork produced at Ugarit in the fourteenth century illustrate Syro-Canaanite art in its best phase of syncretism, or combinations of divergent artistic traditions and styles, with an animal style and filling ornaments which find remarkable parallels in objects from the tomb of Tut-ankh-amun. The figures on a shallow golden bowl from Ras Shamra – winged bulls, eagle-griffins, lions attacking their prey, and vultures flying overhead, as well as a close combat scene between a hero and a lion, whatever their diverse origins – were to become the stock-in-trade of later Phoenician goldsmiths. A second golden bowl from Ras Shamra is embossed with a connected scene of a chariot hunt for bulls. Though cursorily tendered, the scene is one of great action, only to be compared with the Enkomi game-box mentioned below. These were the bowls referred to in the Ugaritic Baal epic: 'bowls for a god, whereon the like of wild beasts of Yemen and wild oxen up to ten thousand are their decoration'.

Ills. 58, 60

No objects of comparable luxury come from the Syro-Hittite region, although a glimpse at beaten metalwork of a more northerly style is given by a gold embossed disk found at Izmir in western Turkey. On this feature

61, 62 Golden bowls from Ras Shamra, fourteenth century BC, are forerunners of Phoenician bowls of later times, but the Canaanites came to prefer formal antithetic themes in decorative zones to the free-field treatment of the chariot-hunt scene

horned demons holding up a sun disk of Hittite form but in a manner typically Hurrian. The beasts and the palm trees, however, compare, except for differences of technique, with those of the more elaborate Ras Shamra bowl, and the piece might be a product of that colony of Hurrian workmen known to be established at Ugarit.

Achaean Cyprus

The closing decades of the thirteenth century were times of great upheaval. Unrest in Anatolia and the North Balkans caused by migration of prehistoric European peoples sent waves of sea-borne invaders into the Levant looking for permanent homes. It was a phenomenon we little understand and which are forced to call vaguely 'the period of the Sea Peoples'. Some of them were probably south-east Europeans – possibly Danubians – but the movement as we see it recorded in Egyptian monuments contained Aegeans and dispossessed Anatolians. Lycians, Phrygians and Thracians established their culture on the ruins of the Late Hittite empire: but Lycians (*Luqqa*) along with Denyen, Philistines (*Plsht*) and other tribes fell on the Levant by sea about 1200 BC and were turned back from the Egyptian Delta in the battle represented

63 Flat bronze figure of a Canaanite dignitary, wearing a prayer-shawl (?), Hazor, 1300 BC

64 Egyptian ships engage the 'Sea Raiders' in the Delta: a relief from the temple of Ramesses III at Medinet Habu, Thebes, *c.* 1170 BC. Note the bird-head prow on the Sea Raider ship, right, the corselets and crested helmets of the Philistines, the horned helmet of the Sherden soldiers (lower right corner), and the Philistine round shields and short swords

on the walls of the temple of Medinet Habu by Ramesses III (*c.* 1170 BC). Many of the Levantine coastal cities appear to have been either depopulated or destroyed.

Cyprus appears to have been least affected by catastrophe, but there the latest phases of the Bronze Age brought successive waves of Mycenaean ('Achaean') colonists from the Greek mainland who replaced the Cypro-Mycenaean pottery tradition with ceramics of the Mycenaean III c 1 Style (1230–1075 BC) and later by the debased 'Granary style' of III c 2 (1075–1025 BC).

These Mycenaeans, together with refugees from coastal Canaanite cities, opened up the copper mines of Cyprus, or *Alasia*, the 'Copper Isle', in the Tell el-Amarna letters. Ingots of a type previously in use in the east Mediterranean and still retaining a memory of primitive barter by being cast in the shape of a bull's hide were apparently exported from the eastern mining centres during the thirteenth century. Exploration of a wrecked Cypriot ship sunk off Cape Gelidonya on the southern Turkish coast in the thirteenth century BC revealed that she was carrying thirty such ingots as well as bronze weapons and agricultural implements. The precise purpose of such ingots is obscure and it certainly cannot be said that they originated in Cyprus, though many bear 'foundry marks' closely

Ills. 47, 48

Ill. 65

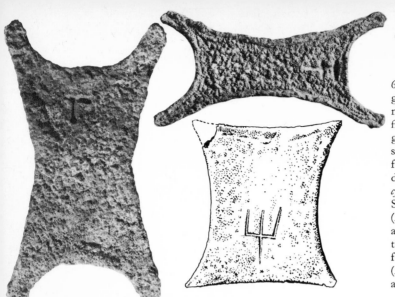

65–67 Ox-hide ingots with foundry marks. Although difficult to classify, generally the narrow shaped ingots, *e.g.* from the Cape Gelidonya wreck (*Ill. 65; cf. Ills. 47, 48*) and Serra Ilixi, Sardinia (*Ill. 66*) are later – about 1200 BC – than the wider examples from Hagia Triada (*Ill. 67*) and Zakro – about 1500 BC

Ill. 46

Ill. 66

Ill. 67

Ill. 68

related to the Bronze Age syllabic script of Cyprus, and Enkomi appears to have been a centre of their production at this later period. Their wide currency in the Levant is shown in Egyptian wall-paintings of Dynasty XVIII in which Syrians and Keftians (Cretans?) are shown bearing considerable numbers of them as tribute. Their distinctive shape appears ideographically used in both Cretan Linear A and Mycenaean Linear B script. Besides their direct value as raw material, they perhaps had the barter value of a primitive currency and thus were acceptable in many of the Levantine markets and even understood in Sardinia and Sicily where examples have been found. Although Syrians bear bull's-hide ingots on Egyptian frescoes, none have been found in Palestine or Syria and it seems likely that they were circulated mainly in the island and Deltaic markets. The earliest examples are from Hagia Triada in Crete, but more recently many have been found in the Late Minoan I palace at Kato Zakro.

Openwork cauldron-stands are also closely associated with the bronze industries of Enkomi, Citium and Ugarit. The earlier simpler versions of these stands, resembling small decorative bronze stools, have been found not only in Cyprus but also in Ras Shamra and Palestine. But a series of larger stands made in Cyprus after 1200 BC,

68–70 Examples of bronze stands. *Ill. 68* right, a bronze openwork cauldron stand is from Curium (?). On each side is a figure: a harpist, a man carrying two tusks, another carrying two fishes, and one bearing an ox-hide ingot. Possibly they are taking tribute into a temple, suggested by the voluted pillar in front of each figure. *Ill. 69* below left, a wheeled stand from Larnaka. The openwork sides show a temple pillar flanked by sphinxes in a manner reminiscent of the 'Lion Gate' at Mycenae. But although the sphinxes themselves have Mycenaean head-gear, the podia beneath their feet suggest rather that they are sphinx statues guarding the entrance to a temple (symbolized by the pillar) – in familiar Near Eastern manner. A similar stand (*Ill. 70* below right) from an unknown site in Cyprus shows Canaanite-like musicians, a sphinx, chariot and a lion on its sides. Simpler Cypriot bronze tripod-stands reached Mycenaean Greece and one is imitated in pottery from a Geometric grave in the Kerameikos, Athens, suggesting a continuation of exports into the ninth century

fitted with wheels and cast in an elaborate openwork of Canaanite and Aegean motifs, appears to correspond to the highly technical description given in *I Kings 7* of the wheeled 'laver stands' made by the Tyrian smiths as part of the ritual equipment for King Solomon's temple. There can be no doubt that motifs such as the sphinxes, banquet and 'soliciting priestess' scene on stands from Citium and Enkomi were still stock themes of the Canaanite artist in Solomon's time and perhaps the smiths who worked in Solomon's employ were descendants of those Canaanites who, three centuries earlier, had founded a workshop in Cyprus. The cauldrons themselves, however, have not been found in Cyprus, and the surprising information of *I Kings* that Solomon's cauldrons were made at a site in the Jordan Valley cannot but be regarded as likely in view of the discovery at Zarethan by Professor J. B. Pritchard of two tombs belonging to a woman of princely family of the twelfth century B C and containing a large bronze cauldron and other vessels as well as a small cauldron-stand of Cypriot or Syrian type. These unaccustomedly wealthy Palestinian burials throw light on the tradition preserved in *I Kings 7, 45–6*: 'Now the pots, the shovels and the basins, all these vessels in the House of the Lord, which King Hiram of Tyre made for Solomon, were of burnished bronze. In the plain of the Jordan the King cast them, in the clay ground between Succoth and Zarethan.'

Despite the general impoverishment of the period, the art of the ivory carver flourished in Cyprus and developed the use of a high relief and polychromy. Carved mirror-handles from Paphos and Enkomi belong to the twelfth century, and one of the best ivories artistically, the game-box from Enkomi now in the British Museum, might be later. The long sides of the game-box show a local Cypro-Canaanite prince hunting bulls from a chariot. Gone is much of the static formality typical of the earlier ivory

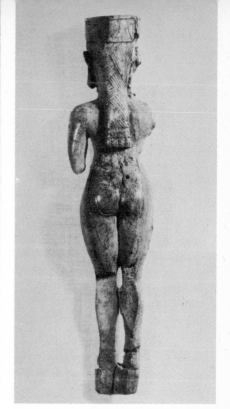

71, 72 Canaanite ivories from Megiddo. The ivory relief female figure (*right*), with her crown and plaited hair is the prototype of similar caryatids from Arslan Tash and Nimrud. The flat fretwork of the 'Canaanite maiden' panel (*left*), compares with the Nimrud piece *Ill. 94*

carving. Instead here is a scene of dynamic action admirably suited to the shape of the box, and probably to the game it was meant to house. The flying gallop of horses and slinking of hounds, the leaping cows and bucking steers, the old bull, shot in the shoulder, making a stubborn stand – all this adds up to a vivacity unattained by any other product of Levantine art. The prince's footman wears the tufted head-dress peculiar to the Philistines. The armed combat between warrior and beast beautifully carved on the mirror-handles appears to be a Mycenaean dressing of a Canaanite theme. These and a few high-relief ivories from Megiddo, here without Mycenaean traits, suggest that a native Canaanite carving style, ancestral to the 'Phoenician ivories' of the next millennium, was already flourishing.

Ills. 71–74

73 Ivory comb from Megiddo: a dog attacks an ibex by the thigh, Although the motif is found in Amarna art, the compact symmetry is un-Egyptian, and is closer to Cypro-Mycenaean ivories (*e.g.* the combat theme on the mirror handles in *Ill. 49*). The design on the upper edge is purely Mycenaean

74 Carved box from Megiddo, made from one piece of ivory with sphinxes and lions carved in high relief. The Egyptian inspiration is here subordinated to Canaanite concepts, and the frontalism of the animals' heads is a device without Egyptian parallel. The stylistic range of the Megiddo ivories, ranging from this Canaanite box to a purely Hittite plaque, suggests that the ivory carver was already aiming at foreign markets

The Philistines

Ill. 75

It is indeed curious that amongst the names of the various ethnic groups composing the Sea Peoples preserved in Egyptian sources, some seem to be connected with the languages of peoples who in the first millennium appear in west Mediterranean lands. Such are the *Shrdn*, tall bearded men with horned helmets (as the Egyptians depicted them) linked perhaps with the later Sardinians; the *Shkl*, with whom the prehistoric Sikels of Sicily have been connected, and the *Trshw* in their tight-fitting caps, perhaps ancestral to the Etruscans of Italy, whom the Greeks called 'Tursenoi'. If these linguistic connections are correct, then we must see amongst the Sea Peoples groups ancestral to western peoples still in a migratory stage before their settlement in western lands, for archaeologically these peoples cannot be identified at this early date.

75 Many colourfully glazed tiles representing the traditional enemies of Egypt were found in the mortuary temple of Ramesses III at Medinet Habu. Left to right are, Nubian, Canaanite, Philistine, Syrian, Nubian, Syrian. They are important evidence for the manufacture of embroidered and patterned cloth in the Levant

The Philistines were a group of these Sea Peoples and the only one that gained permanent settlement in Palestine apart from the small colony of *Tshkr*, on the coast south of Haifa. They occupied the coastal strip between the Carmel peninsula and Gaza and so the Bible affirms, came from Caphtor or Crete. Sweeping into Canaan and into Egypt, attacking the coasts from their high-prowed boats and landing their women and children in ox-drawn carts – so are they pictured about 1175 BC in reliefs on the walls of the Medinet Habu temple built by Ramesses III to celebrate his victory over them in the Nile Delta. The deep footing that they gained on the southern Palestinian coast was probably not without the approval of the Egyptians, who saw in them a satellite power protecting the regular trade routes to the north. Possibly bands of Philistine mercenaries had been settled in Canaan in a last effort to protect Egyptian interests against the Hebrew

Ill. 76

'conquest' which was taking hold of inland Palestine and Galilee in the thirteenth century.

The theory of the Aegean connections of the Philistines is amply supported by archaeological data. Their pottery found in many southern Palestinian sites forms a large and homogeneous group deriving from Late Mycenaean wares. The exact predecessors of this pottery are, however, difficult to determine: its equivalent, not found in Crete, has so far only been found at Sinda in Cyprus, a site near to Enkomi, where also the passage of Philistines is illustrated by graffiti and seals. The Philistine custom of burial in pottery coffins was perhaps developed during a brief sojourn in Egypt or used by mercenaries who had seen service there, although the practice of covering the face of a rich man's corpse with a gold mask is found earlier in the shaft-graves at Mycenae and again in Mycenaean Cyprus.

In the Biblical account the Philistines appear to have had the monopoly of iron working in Canaan and their huge round shields and short stout swords obviously impressed the designer of the Medinet Habu reliefs. Not until the appearance of the Philistines in Palestine does iron become common as a metal for everyday use. The Hittites had used the metal on the shores of the Black Sea before 1300 BC, but its use in the period of the Tell el-Amarna letters was still novel, and an iron dagger and iron rings covered with gold-foil sent by King Tušratta of the Mitannians to Amenophis III were regarded as a precious curiosity. There can be little doubt of the tradition implied in the Bible that it was from Philistines that the Hebrews learned the use of iron. Hebrew words for 'knife' and 'helmet' came from a Philistine or other Aegean source.

During the twelfth century BC, Philistines were placed in strategic positions in the Egyptian army in Egypt, Nubia and Palestine. After Egypt lost power and prestige

76 Prisoners of Ramesses III captured on his campaign in 'Amor' (Amurru) – Libyan, Syrian, Hittite, Sea Peoples, Canaanite. A relief from Medinet Habu *c*. 1170 BC

in Palestine and Syria around the middle of the eleventh century, the Philistines became independent and free to expand their sphere of interest, though by this time they had accepted much of the cultural tradition of Canaan and had ceased to make the pottery which had characterized their presence in the land between 1150 and 1050 BC. This expansion explains the discovery of Philistine levels at sites well outside the Philistine area proper; for example, at Afula (south of Nazareth) and at Gibeah just north of Jerusalem, where Saul pitched his first battle against them.

The cultural influence of Canaan is responsible for the worship of Ishtar and Dagon in the Biblical account of the Philistines, and the excavations at Tell Mor (Ashdod) have revealed the strength of the Canaanite elements in the culture of the flourishing Philistine city in the twelfth century BC. We cannot but be struck, however, by the non-Semitic aspects of Philistine civilization preserved in the Bible: the public games at which Samson was exposed, Goliath's Aegean-type armour, and above all the Aegean-type political confederacy of the Philistine pentapolis – Gaza (Tell el-Ajjul?), Gath (Gattaim?), Ashkelon, Ashdod and Ekron (Tell al-Muqanna?), each ruled by a *seren*, a word thought to be cognate with the Greek *tyrannos*.

Despite the recognizability of Philistine material culture, relatively little is known about Philistine life and trade. The economy was largely based on agriculture, and the Afula evidence suggests that they might have introduced new crop-plants to Palestine. Besides iron and bronze, silver appears to have been available to the Philistine smiths, suggesting overseas contact. At Beth Pelet and other sites, Philistines appear to have followed the Canaanite and Aegean practice of interment in chambered tombs, but important evidence from Azor, a site immediately south-east of Tel Aviv, suggests that various forms of burial were used, perhaps corresponding to the racially mixed elements among 'Sea Peoples'. During the twelfth century, burials at Azor were either simple graves in which the corpse was orientated east–west and accompanied by simple pottery and such simple ornaments as iron armbands, or cist-graves built up of clay bricks. One burial, however, had been made in a crude sarcophagus made of two *pithoi* placed mouth to mouth, a practice paralleled at Kefar Yehoshua in the western part of the Esdraeldon plain, and an important eleventh-century burial was a cremation grave in which the ashes had been placed in an urn surrounded by stone blocks forming an aedicule a metre deep and containing smaller jars, a bronze bowl and a golden mouth covering paralleled in Cyprus and in stratum X at Tell Qasile.

This important evidence corroborates the suggestion that the Sea Peoples included an element which followed

77 Bronze sword from Ras Shamra with the cartouche of Merneptah. Long swords of European type were introduced to Egypt by Sea People mercenaries in the Egyptian army. The Pharaoh Merneptah appears to have attempted to stem the incursion of the Sea Peoples into Syria. Perhaps this sword belonged to his garrison there

the custom of cremation practised in Late Bronze Age Europe and introduced to Greece by the Dorian invaders. Destruction levels corresponding to the invasion of the Sea Peoples in the North Syrian coastal regions are known at Tell Sukas, Atchana and Carchemish, but evidence of resettlement is slight and sporadic. Into the debris of the latest level at Atchana, the newcomers buried their cremated dead in jug-shaped urns surrounded by *loculi* of stones: at Carchemish the later post-destruction period is known from the cremation graves of the Yunus cemetery. Some time after the reign of Merneptah (*c.* 1220 BC), Ugarit too was destroyed: a sword with his engraved cartouche is one of the latest datable objects from the city's final period. Ugarit, like the Syrian cities in general, was left unoccupied by her conquerors and, unlike the cities from Lebanon southwards, which were soon to flourish once more, she remained lost in a Dark Age until reopened to Greek trade in the first millennium.

Ill. 77

The half-mythical, half-historical travelogue of the Egyptian Wen-Amun, written about 1070 BC, gives some account of the conditions of trade at that period as the banding together of impoverished individuals or states to form trade syndicates. In one of these syndicates Sidon is mentioned for the first time the 'Fisher Town', which gradually rose to power in the first millennium and in the period reflected by the compositions of Homer had entirely eclipsed Byblos, which in the time of Wen-Amun's visit still held some form of dominance over the other coastal towns. To Homer, however, Sidon and the Sidonians became synonymous with all that was 'Phoenician', the name given by the Greeks to the people of the modern Lebanese seaboard.

CHAPTER FOUR

Phoenicia and Israel

Before the rise of the city of Sidon, and little over a century after Wen-Amun's visit, Tyre, called Sidon's daughter in the book of Isaiah, had risen to maritime prominence and was probably head of the carrying trade. The origin of both these cities, and indeed the origin of Phoenician civilization generally, is lost, for neither excavations nor written documents throw much light on the eleventh and tenth centuries B C. It is indeed possible that the birth of 'Phoenicia' was brought about by the formation of a new population group composed mainly of sea-raider settlers and coastal Canaanites. The role of Phoenicia in early first millennium trade is known to us chiefly from the Bible.

It was under David that young Israel achieved its maximum territorial extent and for a brief period became a major Near Eastern power. Of David's campaigns against the Philistines culminating in the victory at Mizpah (*I Sam. VII*) full details are preserved in the Biblical record, but a more formidable, if less immediate threat to David's realm was the occupation by a new wave of Semitic nomads, the Aramaeans, of the lands on the western periphery of central and northern Syria. It was by his defeat of Hadadezer of Aram Zobah at the battle of Helam that David was led to occupy the former

Aramaean territories, stretching in the north to the Euphrates and to the borders of the kingdom of Hamath, whose king Toi appears to have become a vassal. Solomon was able for many years to maintain this northern empire which gave Israel control of the main caravan routes across Syria to the coast as well as the Transjordanian routes to Arabia and Aqabah. Solomon appears to have used Hamath as an entrepôt in the overland trade from South Anatolia, including the importation of horses from Cilicia. Whilst undoubtedly the rapid expansion of Israel was in part due to the weakness of the contemporary dynasties in Assyria and Egypt, it speaks well for Solomon's military strength that he was apparently able to repel an Egyptian attempt to gain control of Philistia on David's death and to make a pact with the Pharaoh Si-amun whereby the latter ceded the stronghold of Gezer, possibly the last Egyptian garrison in Philistia, and the hand of his daughter in a diplomatic marriage.

Although King Solomon could not maintain his grip on the territories conquered by David, his policies in Israel were greatly enhanced by an economic alliance with Tyre. With the aid of Phoenician masons and craftsmen new cities and citadels were built throughout Palestine, and the prosperity of the second half of the tenth century has left a distinctive archaeological record. The most northerly evidence of Solomonic building is at Ein Gev on the eastern side of the Sea of Galilee, astride the old route from Damascus to the coast, but it is also possible that the stratum E buildings at Hamath are connected with Solomon's activities there. On Israel's southern extremity a farming settlement at Ramat Matred in the Negev appears to be linked with expansion under Solomon. But the distinctive features of Solomonic architecture, the beautifully drafted masonry, casemate walls and pilasters are best seen inside Palestine at Hazor, Megiddo and Gezer, dating either from the period of Solomon himself

78 Late Bronze Age temple, Area H. Hazor, consisting of a porch, central room and sanctuary. Other Canaanite temples employ a basic three-room plan, but without any consistent layout

(as does stratum X at Hazor) or to the times of later monarchs who maintained the traditions of 'royal architecture' initiated under Solomon. The discoveries come as a striking witness to the statement in *I Kings 9, 15*: 'And this is the reason of the levy which King Solomon raised; for to build the house of the Lord and his own house, and Millo, and the wall of Jerusalem and Hazor and Megiddo and Gezer.' There is little doubt that at all four cities Solomon's highly skilled corps of masons worked to prepared specifications and plans. So impressed was Solomon by the layout of the temples of Melqart at Tyre that he commissioned the Tyrian king Hiram to construct the Jerusalem temple on similar lines. Certain features of Solomon's Temple, as described in the Book of Kings, have been compared to those of the Late Bronze Age temple in Area H at Hazor, especially the twin cultic pillars (Jachin and Boaz in the Bible) set before the entrance to the middle room. Recently a building similar

Ill. 78

79, 80 This 'Proto-Aeolic' volute capital from Hazor, like others used in Israelite royal architecture, was derived from the sacred palm design, as seen on the eighth-century ivory pyxis from Nimrud (*right*)

to the Hazor temple in many details has been found in south-east Judaea in the tenth-century level at Tel Arad, a flourishing export centre of Dead Sea products in Solomon's day, dominating the routes to Eilat and the Arabah. No traces of Solomon's buildings have survived in Jerusalem. The artificial platform (or 'Millo') which he built on the threshing floor of Araunah was on the north of the Late Bronze ('Jebusite') settlement on Ophel and is probably somewhere below the enlarged platform built for the Herodian temple in the present Haram-esh-Sharif. In recent excavations on Ophel, Miss Kenyon unearthed dressed blocks and a pillar capital of proto-Aeolic form, elsewhere associated with 'royal architecture'. Possibly this was part of a Solomonic retaining wall of the Millo.

Following the division of Solomon's territories into two kingdoms, it was the northern kingdom of Israel which maintained closest contact with Phoenicia. In the reigns of kings Omri and Ahab (*c.* 880–850 BC) important trade routes between Phoenicia and Transjordanian Aramaean and Ammonite territory passed through Israel (now the name of the northern kingdom) and commercial relations between Omri and Ithobaal of Tyre led to the marriage of Ahab and the Phoenician princess Jezebel. The capital built by Omri at Samaria (the only major town founded by the Israelites) continued the Solomonic tradition in architecture and featured proto-Aeolic capitals with two curling lotus volutes. Similar capitals, ancestral to the Greek Ionic order, have been found in stratum IV at Megiddo, at Hazor, and in Cyprus. The tradition was continued in Judah (the southern kingdom), where the

81 This hellenized stela from Golgoi, Cyprus, demonstrates the survival of the Phoenician volute capital there. Sixth century BC

75

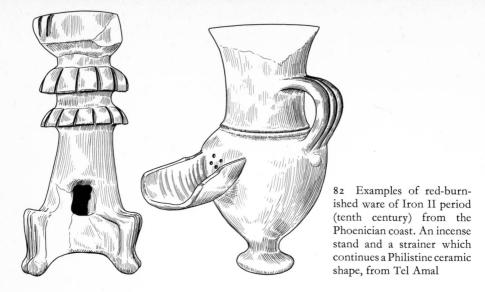

Ill. 82

82 Examples of red-burn-
ished ware of Iron II period
(tenth century) from the
Phoenician coast. An incense
stand and a strainer which
continues a Philistine ceramic
shape, from Tel Amal

palace probably built by King Uzziah at Ramat Rachel
is a minor work of royal style.

The influence of Phoenicia was even more apparent in
pottery. The tenth and ninth centuries brought into use
in the Israelite cities elegant crimson burnished jugs and
bowls sometimes known as 'Samaria Ware', but which
appear to have been originally produced by the Phoenicians of Lebanon. At the same time Cypro-Phoenician
Iron Age wares, especially the elegant little juglets of
black-on-red ware and other geometric fabrics, are found
at Syrian and Palestinian sites. The entire Levant was
beginning to be opened up by Phoenician traders.

Israel too now made an appearance as a maritime
nation, largely in co-operation with Tyrian enterprise. It
is not known how much control David and Solomon
gained over the Philistine seaboard cities; most probably
the region south of the tribal territory of Dan was never
fully subdued. But on the northern edge of Philistine
territory an Israelite port was established at Tell Qasile
on the Yarkon river within the modern boundaries of
Tel Aviv. Here the earliest settlement was of Philistine
origin, but the eleventh–tenth-century level was a flourishing Israelite settlement with large public buildings and
storehouses and pottery links with Phoenicia and Cyprus.

83 'Gold of Ophir for Beth Horon, shekels III'; inscription on a potsherd from Tell Qasile, an ancient port on the South Palestine coast. The gold was perhaps intended as tribute for a near-by shrine of the Canaanite god Horon, a derivative of the Egyptian Harakhti. About 700 BC

Ophir and Tarshish

The Book of Kings and chapter XXVII of Ezekiel acquaint us with that far-flung trade of Tyre in the ninth and eighth centuries which reached Egypt and Arabia and even beyond. Hiram of Tyre was able, with Solomon's assistance, to build a trading fleet at Ezion-geber (Eilat) on the shores of the Gulf of Aqaba. Nelson Glueck's report on Ezion-geber gives clear evidence of shipping activities, although no remains of the port itself were found. Of much interest are the large copper and iron nails and remains of caulking pitch and ships' rope. Oak planks from timber cut in the forest of the hills of Edom furnished the Phoenician craftsmen with the basic material for boat-building as well as providing fuel for a copper refinery active, as is shown by seals, in the days of the Judaean kings Jehosaphat (860 BC) and Jotham (740 BC) and almost certainly dating back to Solomon's day. The main object of these expeditions was to obtain gold, precious woods and incense from Ophir. From the recent discovery at Tell Qasile of a storage jar inscribed in cursive Phoenician script 'Gold of Ophir', historical substance is given to a land hitherto thought to be legendary. It was almost certainly one of the south Arabian principalities which rose to commercial prominence during the

Ill. 83

early part of the first millennium. In fact, South Arabia was probably the wealthiest area of the Semitic world at this period as is attested by the rich architectural remains of the Qatabanian and Sabaean cities. This wealth was largely brought about by the increased demand for commodities which only Arabia and Somaliland could supply – frankincense and myrrh, produced by trees native to this region. Much of the trade in incense passed northwards to the fertile crescent by overland routes and it was probably in connection with trade relations that the Queen of Saba (Sheba) visited Solomon, through whose territory the caravans must pass. But the carrying trade along the gulf ports was also developed and Ezion-geber developed as the transhipment point for goods destined for caravans for Phoenicia. The northern merchants brought with them northern tastes, and the surviving examples of Qatabanian and Sabaean art seem to be heavily influenced by Phoenician taste.

Whilst these Ophir voyages from Ezion-geber, revived under the Judaean king Jeroboam II, opened a new era of eastern exploration, it is doubtful that they went farther than Dhufar on the Arabian coast. The gold, ivory, apes and peacocks brought back by the Phoenician fleet from Ophir (*I Kings 10–22*) suggest that they had traded farther afield with India, but the Hebrew words for peacocks (*thukkiyīm*) and ivory (*šenhabbīm*) are of doubtful age in this text and even if *thukkiyīm* is derived from the Dravidic Indian word *toka*, peacock – other derivations are possible – it does not prove the identity of Ophir and India. It is indeed more likely that the India passage was reopened by the later Babylonian merchants whose forebears had made contact with the Indus valley. In 695 B C, Sennacherib had a fleet constructed by Phoenician merchants on the Persian Gulf to strike at the soft underbelly of Babylon against whose king, Merodach Baladan, he was engaged in war. It is possible that on completion of their military

84 The cartouche on this ivory plaque from Nimrud appears to name Iaubidi, the king of Hamath about 720 BC. Phoenician inscriptions on the backs of the ivories identify two Northern Syrian states – Hamath and Laash

duties these ships were turned to commerce. All that we know is that the cotton trees ('trees that bear fleece') were introduced by Sennacherib to Assyria about 700 BC and that the Assyrians began to eat rice about the same time. It is possible, of course, that the trading impulses came from India herself.

Phoenician Ivories

The quest for ivory in Tarshish illustrates the importance of this material for Phoenician artists in the ninth and eighth centuries. Not until the ferment caused by the incursions of the Philistines from the west and the Hebrews and Aramaeans from the east had settled, was the Syro-Palestinian region able to revive its late second millennium tradition in carving. It is clear that the groups of carved ivories found at several Near Eastern sites and especially at Shalmaneser's capital at Nimrud belong to different schools, but this does not necessarily mean that they were the products of several centres. The concentration of finds of carved ivories in North Syria and North Mesopotamia has long been taken to indicate that the workshop or bazaar was near the source of ivory – the Syrian elephant. This now appears to have been Hamath; not only has the word *Hmt* been found on the back of one of the Nimrud ivories, but R. D. Barnett has argued that a royal name written in Egyptian hieroglyphs on one of the Nimrud group stands for Iaubidi, king of Hamath in 720 BC. Ivories from Arslan Tash in North Syria appear to have been made for Hazael, king of Damascus in the

Ill. 84

Ills. 85, 86

85, 86 Ivories from Arslan Tash (North Syria) receive both naturalistic and formal treatment. The cow licking her calf symbolized the love of the mother goddess for her offspring. The sphinx, despite its typically Phoenician greyhound-like body, takes its stiffness from Egypt. Note the erratic representation of Egyptian headgear. Ninth century BC

87 In this high relief, ▷ the finest of the Nimrud ivories, a lioness has caught a negro boy in a thicket

88, 89   A contrast of styles in the ivories from Nimrud. The 'Egyptian' goddess Isis, here guarding panels of hieroglyphs, later lent her iconography to the Carthaginian Tanit. The young bearded god, in North Syrian style, plucking fruit from the sacred tree is perhaps Tammuz, who, in his Carthaginian form, Eshmun, is represented in Punic terracotta male heads with beards and close-set curls

ninth century B C. Egyptian, Aramaean, Cypriot, Phoenician – all these influences appear in the ivories, and probably the staff of the bazaar was recruited from many sources, with Phoenicia foremost. But in spite of this mixed inspiration and artistic tradition, their carvers managed to achieve a synthesis which is itself creative, and to express a refined and typically Phoenician taste.

Ills. 88, 89, 94

Ill. 87

Excellent ivories from Nimrud, here illustrated, retain remains of coloured inlay and gold with which parts of the ivories, particularly the clothing, were covered. Some of them, even in their present fragmentary state, are masterpieces; such as the ivory scene of the lion devouring the curly haired boy in a thicket of reeds. Other pieces, such as those in openwork showing designs of hinds browsing on lilies or comely maidens gathering flowers, have a delicate simplicity often compared with verses from the Book of Psalms, whose imagery they could sometimes well illustrate. Even the 'Soliciting

90 The 'woman at the window' was a favourite motif of the ivory carver. Though its interpretation is doubtful, most probably it represents the temple prostitute, the substitute of her mistress Ashtart, soliciting from her upper window. Nimrud, eighth century BC

Astarte', a fertility theme in which a female face stares through a half-open window, is treated without crudity.

Ill. 90

For the history of art the ivories have an importance which reaches beyond the Levantine world. Many of them are masterpieces of naturalistic carving such as was not achieved in other materials and their production was on a large scale. The classical Biblical reference is Ahab's 'ivory house' at Samaria, where ivories related to those of Nimrud have been unearthed. But we read of the Assyrian king Ashurnasirpal receiving a tribute of ivory and elephants from 'all Phoenicia' and in the loot taken from Damascus by Adadnirari III (806–782 BC) are listed beds and stools of ivory from the royal palace. Sargon is said to have a palace of ivory and even Hezekiah of Judah was able to send raw and worked ivory in tribute to Sennacherib in 701 BC. The sources of this great quantity of ivory can only have been partly local, for the native Syrian elephants were becoming scarce in the first

Ills. 91–93

91–93   The themes of the Samaria ivories are mostly Egyptian derivitives. *Ill. 91* above, shows a panel on which winged figures fan the *djed* pillar. In *Ill. 92* the young Egyptian god Horus sits upon the primaeval lotus. The cherub-sphinx of *Ill. 93* retains a vestigial Egyptian royal crown but is Syrian in all details

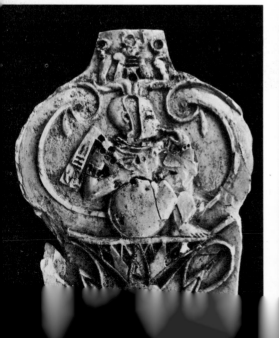

Openwork ivory panel of a lion in a lily grove from Nimrud. The head-dress is that of the Egyptian lion-goddess Sekhmet and the breast-plate that of Hathor. The cable border, common in the Orient, spread to Greece and Italy in the Orientalizing period

95 Many ivories at Nimrud are distinctly Assyrian in style and are probably the work of local shops set up in emulation of the Phoenicians. Ivories from Ziwiyeh, Iran, include this example of a mature Assyrian style of about 650 BC

millennium BC. Consequently the guilds of Phoenician ivory carvers must have prospected the sources of the Sudan and North Africa in order to keep up with the demands on their workshops now established in parts of the Assyrian empire, for the Nimrud ivories were in part locally carved by Phoenicians, and there is plenty of evidence that their work gave rise to a local Assyrian-style product. None of the ivories antedates the reign of Ashurnasirpal (883–859 BC), the first Assyrian king to maintain close contact with the Phoenician coast.

It was not only in west Asiatic courts that 'Phoenician' ivories were prized. The kings of Urartu followed Assyrian fashion as can be seen in the ivories from Toprakkale (Van), and fine ivory harness fittings were found recently in a Phrygian tomb at Gordium (central Turkey) dating to the end of the eighth century and later pieces at Ziwiyeh in Iran. But, above all, the ivories reached the Greek world. Pilgrims dedicated them in the shrine of Mount Ida in Crete and at the temple of Hera on Samos; other examples reached Rhodes. These provide examples of that seventh-century love of exotic Oriental objects which began in Greece that period known as 'Orientalizing', which, through classical art, has left its legacy to our own times. 'Phoenician Art' can be applied to these ivories only in the widest sense for a second Semitic group, the northern branch of the Aramaeans became an important influence in the first millennium.

Aramaean States in Syria

After the break-up of the great Hittite Empire in the late second millennium, a number of small city-states had grown up in the Ceyhan valley, the Marash plain, the Upper Euphrates valley with Syrian extensions in the Amuq plain and about Aleppo. Of these the chief was Carchemish, a stronghold of the Empire on the Euphrates which maintained much of its Hittite character. Other

96　A further local style, inspired indirectly by the Phoenician craft, is seen in this ivory from Ziwiyeh showing figures in local Iranian dress

cities, however, in which the basic Hittite population had been gradually outnumbered by immigrant Aramaeans, were strongly Semitic, and for a period the official language at Sinjerli, as at Karatepe, was Phoenician. At this latter site a long bilingual inscription in Hittite hieroglyphs and Phoenician script has been an important key in understanding the Hittite language. The appearance of Phoenician in such a remote area may be explained by the employment by the Aramaeans of artists and engravers from among their Phoenician kindred. In other cities such as Marash, Carchemish and Tell Tainat, the Anatolian element predominated and Hittite was spoken. As these city-states were buffers between Assyria and the central Anatolian kingdoms, Assyrian influence was varyingly felt.

The artistic expression of these Syro-Hittite cities was an amalgam of Phoenician, Aramaean, Assyrian and Hittite styles and was somewhat unified by the practice they adopted of decorating their royal palaces with dados carved in low relief as can be seen on the façade of the

97, 98 The earliest outstanding monument of Aramaean art is the Temple-Palace at Tell Halaf, which predates the beginning of Assyrian domination of the region in 808 BC. The Caryatid porch (*right*), has been reconstructed in Berlin and the inscription on the Caryatid figure (*left*), names the 'Palace of Kaparu son of Hadianu'

Ills. 97, 98

Temple Palace of Tell Halaf in North Syria. Tell Halaf was the capital of the Assyrian-dominated province of Guzana. The Temple Palace (a building that combined secular with religious functions) was rebuilt and decorated with a sculptured dado by King Kaparu in the second half of the ninth century, and his name and those of his father and grandfather are given in cuneiform on the skirt of the woman and the left shoulders of the two men who form the pillars supporting the architrave. Like the Phoenician ivories, it contains a mixture of motifs as do also the sculptures from Sinjerli and Carchemish, which are especially valuable for their wealth of detail in dress and accoutrements. The daily life of a people mixed in origin yet remarkably homogeneous in their material culture is here more fully illustrated than anywhere else in the Levant in the early first millennium. Scenes of hunting from chariot and on foot, fowling and trapping, the royal banquet, a girls' band, a party for two, and a

99 A steatite carving industry was active in North Syria. Its most widely traded products were spoon-like 'pipe bowls' like this from Carchemish. They are carved with lions, elaborate palms, and sometimes the open human hand, which suggests that their use, though strictly unknown, was connected with tending ritual fires. Eighth century BC

school lesson are examples of the repertoire. An important feature of Syro-Hittite art is its interest in carved lions, vigorous snarling beasts which were admired and copied by Greek artists of the seventh century.

Ill. 99

The influence of the style can be seen in a set of bronze shields from Mount Ida in Crete. From a late-ninth-century grave from the Kerameikos cemetery in Athens comes a beaten bronze bowl which has both Syro-Hittite and Cypriot characteristics. Other bronze bowls found in Greece at Delphi and Olympia have a Phoenician repertoire of lions and skirted sphinxes executed in a rather Assyrian manner and paralleled in a bronze bowl from Nimrud. These examples should be assigned to the mid-eighth century, whilst a fragmentary bowl of similar style from a grave at Fortetsa in Crete and of a more distinctively Phoenician decoration cannot be closely dated from its context. In addition, a number of bronze and golden bowls are known from Cyprus. These as a rule employ deep incision alongside beaten technique and dispose the decoration, rich in mythological content, in three friezes round the circumference. The Cypriot bowls, the style of which allows us to imagine more clearly the work of Phoenician coastal workshops in the eighth century, are lineal descendants of the fourteenth-century Ras Shamra bowls. The Delphi and Olympia bowls on the other hand probably represent the metalworking tradition of a Syrian centre influenced by late Egyptian works. Other 'Phoenician' metalwork, metal attachments for harness, come from Cyprus, Rhodes and Samos and to some extent copy earlier ivory trappings found at Nimrud. A bronze horse

Ill. 100

100 Bronze bowls from Nimrud belong to differing styles, some more Syrian and showing Assyrian influences; some more properly Phoenician. This Nimrud bowl is engraved in a formal pseudo-Egyptian Phoenician style

frontal from Tell Tainat decorated with three figures has a precise parallel at Samos and appears to be North Syrian work whilst plaques showing animal combats recently found at Olympia have Iranian elements in their decoration.

The Greeks in the East

After the collapse of Mycenaean power, recovery of Greek interest in the east was slow. During the Protogeometric and Geometric periods of Greek prehistory, relations with the Levant remained broken. The years between 1050 and 950 BC are still an obscure 'Dark Age' in the history of the western Asiatic maritime countries, and a firm chronology cannot be built up from either historical or archaeological sources. They appear to have been years of general unrest and impoverishment.

As regards the Greeks, their reopening of eastern trade about 800 BC introduced one of the most significant periods in the history of western civilization. Not only did the east become a fresh source of artistic inspiration but also its accumulated knowledge was opened to the west; astronomical data, materia medica, mathematical and legal concepts, with all their content of Oriental superstition, now became available to the logical and speculative minds of the Greeks and the wealth of Oriental legend and mythology subject to Greek literary forms.

Sherds of pottery skyphoi with geometric decoration of concentric semicircles are the first evidence of trade revival. They occur at a number of sites but in small quantity: Tell Abu Hawam and Ashkelon on the Palestine coast; Tell Sukas, Al Mina, Tabhat el-Hammam, Hama, Tell Halaf in North Syria; Cyprus, and at Tarsus and Mersin in Cilicia. Skyphoi of this type, usually classified as 'Cycladic Geometric' wares, are difficult to date, but their apogee appears to have been 800–750 BC, though possibly they began half a century earlier. Euboea rather than the Cyclades is regarded by some authorities as the home of this pottery, and it is possible that Euboean Chalcis played a leading part in founding a colony at Al Mina, Greek Posideion, at the mouth of the Orontes. In levels 7–5 at Al Mina the geometric wares give place to dark-glazed East Greek 'Ionian' skyphoi with simple reserve or painted bands on the shoulder. Most probably they originated in Rhodes, and at Al Mina and other sites they are accompanied by Rhodian 'bird-bowls', which lasted from about 725 to 600 BC. These Rhodian ceramics are generally much rarer on the central and southern coasts of Palestine, but at Mezad Hashavyahu near Jaffa, as at Tell Sukas, the East Greek vessels are accompanied by *Ill. 106* Rhodian vases painted in the wild goat style of about 600 BC. At Tell Sukas (Greek Paltos) a colony appears to have established a local pottery whose wares were exported to the Amuq sites.

101, 102 Phoenicia's exoticism, as known to Greek eyes, is exemplified in the bichrome pottery of Cyprus eighth to seventh centuries BC. Interestingly, the vase-painter – probably also the weaver – used purple paint, exotic birds and palm trees; the Greek word 'phoenix' denoted all three. The red burnished juglet in *Ill. 102* is a ware typical of coastal Phoenicia, and bears the owner's name in Phoenician script

103–105   Although Phoenicians were credited in antiquity with the invention of glass, they merely copied Egyptian techniques. However, with the suitable fine sand of their estuaries, they developed a glass industry in the first millennium. *Ill. 103* shows the Disney-like polychrome glass beads which were a Phoenician speciality, widely exported. Coloured glass-pastes were used to inlay jewellery in twelfth century B C Cyprus, the inlaid sceptre (*Ill. 104*) comes from Curium and *Ill. 105* shows a typical sand-core glass bottle

106 Rhodes had close links with the Levant. This amphora in the distinctive Rhodian 'wild goat style' (650–600 BC) was found at Tell Sukas (Syria) and the sherds at Mezad Hashavyahu (Israel)

It is very difficult to be precise about the origins of the Oriental influences which inspired the 'Orientalizing period' (730–630 BC) of the Aegean area. Contact with the Orient was not limited to the north-eastern corner of the Mediterranean, for by this time the Greeks, especially the Milesians, had colonized the Black Sea and Pontic region and were in contact with the Vannic kingdom of Urartu and the mountain highlands of northwestern Persia. Similarly, the Ionian Greeks were in overland contact with Phrygia and Lydia, the heirs to Hittite culture. But it was certainly through the North Syrian ports that the influences of Syro-Hittite art and Phoenician ivories travelled and Persian metalwork and Elamite embroidered fabrics brought by the overland caravans were exported.

With the general problems of the trade routes with the Orient is connected the problem of Urartian exports to the west, not only to Greece but also to Crete and Etruria. It has been assumed that the campaigns of Sargon II against Urartu brought about the settlement

94

of refugee metalworkers in North Syria and even in Crete, but it appears more likely that lines of export from Urartu, overland, across Asia Minor to Samos and south-westwards to the North Syrian ports, brought the typical Urartian cauldrons to the west, and that this trade was not seriously affected by Assyrian interference. It is, however, of great significance that Urartu dominated the Syro-Hittite states throughout the first half of the eighth century and added yet a further component to the stylistic mixture of Syro-Hittite culture. Urartian cauldrons and their stands had an important influence on the metalwork of Italy, Greece and, indirectly, Europe.

107 Metalware products of Urartu reached the West through non-Phoenician channels and influenced Etruscan and European smiths. Cauldrons like this from Altintepe (eastern Anatolia) have been found in Italy at Cumae and Vetulonia, whilst their handle-attachments or tripod-legs have appeared in Cyprus, Rhodes, Samos, Greece and Italy. Eighth to seventh centuries BC

108 Imaginary reconstruction of a Cypro-Phoenician lady at her toilet, about 650 BC. The architectural setting makes use of details from extant tomb structures and ivories; the clothing and adornment come from terracotta models like *Ill. 114*

The Phoenicians and their Colonies

The decline of the Philistine culture on the Palestinian coast and the growth of a distinctive Israelite culture inland in the second phase of the Iron Age (1000-840 BC) appear to have provided conditions of a certain cultural unity on the Levantine coastal strip. This we should describe as Phoenician. It is best seen at such sites as Tell Qasile and Ashdod where its distinctive feature is the wealth of Cypriot pottery. Recent exploration at Ashdod, an old Philistine settlement, unearthed a ninth-century shrine consisting of several rooms, the main room provided with a large altar around which were found ritual vessels and figurines. This valuable discovery only serves, however, to highlight our ignorance of the archaeology of Phoenicia during this important period, especially of Tyre and Sidon.

Ill. 109

Ill. 110

The rise of Tyre as a major maritime power had important consequences in the Mediterranean basin. After Mycenae, Tyre became the second colonial power in the Levant, colonizing Cyprus and by the foundation of Utica, Cadiz and Carthage establishing permanent colonies in the west Mediterranean.

It is generally assumed that the Phoenicians arrived in Cyprus some time after the Mycenaeans. As we have seen, Canaanite interest in the 'copper isle' goes back to

Places on the map (reading as labelled):

Cape Gelidonya · Mersin · Tarsus · Karatepe · Marash · Sinjerli · Carchemish · Arslan Tash · Tell Fecheriyeh · Tell Halaf · CEYHAN · AMANUS MTS · AMUQ · HATAY · Tell Tainat · Atchana · Al Mina · Aleppo · BALIH · Ras Shamra · Jebleh · Tell Sukas · ORONTES · Hamath · EUPHRATES · ALAŠIA · Enkomi · Sinda · Citium · Paphos · Curium · Arwad · NAHR EL-KEBIR · Qatna · Kadesh · Byblos · LEBANON MTS · BEQAA · ANTI-LEBANON · Sidon · Sarepta · Damascus · Tyre · ARAM-ZOBAH · Achzib · Hazor · Ein Gev · Tell Abu Hawam · Athlit · Megiddo · Samara · Zarethan · Tel Qasile · Mezad Hashavyahu · Tell Farah · Gezer · Jericho · Ashdod · Jerusalem · Ashkelon · Tell Gath · Ramat Rachel · Gaza · Lachish · Nahal Mishmar · Beth Pelet · Tel Arad · NEGEV · Avaris · Tell el-Yehudîyeh · NILE · GULF OF SUEZ · GULF OF AQABA · Ezion-geber · Lahun · Gurob · Serabit el-Khadem

Scale:
0 — 100 — 200 Miles
0 — 100 — 200 — 300 Kilometres

109 Map of the Levant showing main sites

the thirteenth century and is perhaps earlier, but direct evidence for the permanent establishment of Phoenician colonies is lacking before the eighth century BC unless we accept an inscribed tombstone dated on the grounds of its inscription to the first half of the ninth. This tombstone merely records the burial of a Phoenician in the

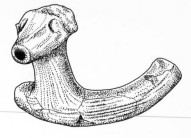
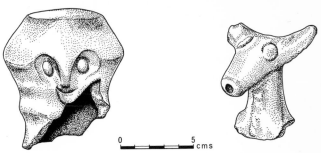

110 Pottery from a shrine at post-Philistine Ashdod includes circular libation vessels with theriomorphic spouts, remotely derived from Mycenaean ceramics. Animal-spouted libation vases occur among Carthaginian pottery. Ninth to eighth centuries BC

unknown locality of 'Cape Eshmun', but an inscription on an eighth-century bronze bowl found near Amathus reads: 'Governor at Kartihadesht, servant of Hiram, King of the Sidonians.'

It seems that the Phoenician tributary kingdoms of Cyprus were already in existence in the late eighth century. Indeed the Jewish historian Josephus takes us back almost thus far when he records that Citium broke away in revolt from Elulaios of Tyre, who appears to have been the Luli of Assyrian inscriptions who successfully withstood the attack of Shalmaneser V about 727 BC. Kartihadesht, 'Carthage' or 'New City' founded at Citium (Larnaka) near the old Mycenaean site, was the most important of these 'daughters of Tyre'. In later times Phoenician dynasties are known to have ruled in Idalium and Citium. Whilst it is difficult to distinguish Phoenician from native pottery at this period the appearance in the south-eastern region of the island of red-slipped and burnished juglets of 'Samaria ware' type and black-on-red flasks which now become common both in the Lebanon and Cyprus can be taken as evidence of close contact, if not colonization, between Cyprus and Phoenicia from about 950 BC.

Discoveries of Phoenician tombs at Athlit and more recently at Achzib, south of Tyre, have made us more familiar with both the pottery and burial customs of the Phoenicians of a later period (800–600 BC). The ceramic connections with Cyprus remained close, but the distinctive Phoenician disk-top jug and burial jar diverge from Cypriot types. Characteristic of these graves is the use of cremation and inhumation side by side. At Achzib, corpses and urns of ashes were placed in rock-hewn tombs, the ashes with scraps of jewellery rescued from the pyre, the corpses occasionally fitted with a miniature terracotta mask. Similar cremation burials have been found at Qrayeh (Lebanon), Rechidyeh (Tyre) and Beth Pelet (South Palestine) and are paralleled in at least one tomb from Larnaka. Cypriot black-on-red ware from the Phoenician sphere was exported both to Crete and Rhodes, and in Arkades and Fortetsa cemeteries, both of the Orientalizing period, the influence of other Phoenician pottery shapes was strong, even though the ceramics of Phoenicia proper appear to have been of little aesthetic distinction at this time. We can only assume that patterns were transmitted on fabrics and this appears most likely the case in the rich repertory of patterns found on the Fortetsa pottery, many of which appear distinctively Phoenician.

Cyprus

The cross-fertilization of Greek and Phoenician culture in Cyprus between the eighth and sixth centuries caused the latent Cypriot flower of fantasy to break into extravagant bloom. Comical painted birds, singing strings of Z's (the earliest known attempt at recording musical notes), appear on the bichrome pottery along with capering goats, human-headed sheep and a fantastic arboretum of curly palm trees. The painting tradition is a development of late Cypro-Mycenaean tradition but the palms and

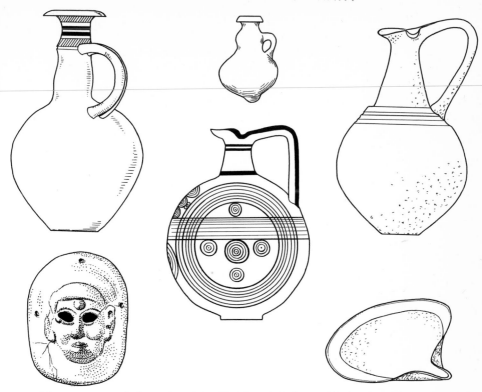

111 These grave-goods from Phoenician burials at Achzib provide the closest known parallels to Punic tomb equipment. Here, as at Carthage and elsewhere, the piriform jug and the mushroom-top flask are the main ceramic types, and miniature terracotta masks were sometimes placed in the tomb. Eighth century BC

dish-palmettes, goats and sphinxes are of Phoenician origin and the scenes chosen to decorate shallow dishes and plates show a close acquaintance with Phoenician beaten metalwork.

Whilst of the homeland Phoenicians we have few surviving monuments, of the Cypro-Phoenician culture we have a wealth of detail bequeathed in painting, terracotta modelling and statuary. It is difficult to say how much of this exotic culture was typical of Phoenicia herself, although its preoccupation with details give it an intimate femininity more Phoenician than Greek.

In the terracotta models, some of which are genre scenes of daily life such as women baking bread, having a bath or washing at a communal laundry, and from the limestone sculptures we obtain an idea of rich racial diversity of features and types of dress, varying from the cunning-faced Cypro-Greeks to those of the bland Cypro-Phoenicians. Other statues, found near Arsos, depict a fat-faced group which fit into neither category. Enough real treasure has survived from Cypriot tombs to show that in the arts of cosmetic and jewellery, for both men and women, Cyprus led the Levant for three centuries: many details of male and female dress and jewellery can be reconstructed from vase paintings and terracotta and, although no buildings survive, a number of built lime-stone tombs, preserved mouldings and other details employed in better-class Phoenician domestic architecture.

Of particular note are the tumulus burials in the necropolis of ancient Salamis investigated in 1957 and 1962. Here wealthy aristocrats of this prominent Graeco-Phoenician city of Cyprus had their cremated ashes laid to rest in chamber tombs reminiscent of those of both Mycenaean and Ugaritic tradition, but dating to the early seventh century BC. The pottery is of the Cypriot archaic

112 Gold crowns made up of hinged plaques were worn by Phoenician ladies. This pair is of unknown provenance. The tubular hinges are a specific feature of Phoenician work. Eighth century BC

113, 114 The Phoenician shrine of Ashtart at Paphos, shown on this gold medallion, became famous amongst Greeks and the richly adorned priestesses of her cult are often represented among Cypriot Iron Age terracottas (*right*)

period decorated with geometric bichrome designs, but horse trappings of Phoenician type and a golden Phoenician bowl were placed among the grave-goods as well as stamped gold-foils belonging to a Cypriot class of Phoenician goldwork. Following a custom described by Homer and which may have been introduced to Cyprus from Greece by the Achaean colonists of Late Mycenaean times, the slaves and horses of the deceased prince were slaughtered and buried in the *dromos* of the tomb along with his chariot and other possessions.

The Western Phoenicians

By Greek tradition, which is untrustworthy since it tended to exaggerate the importance of the Phoenicians as forerunners of their own colonies, the foundation of the far-western cities was placed very early; 1110 BC in the case of Cadiz, 1100 for Utica. Archaeological proof for

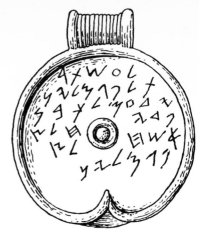

115, 116 Phoenician inscription from Nora (Cape Pula), Sardinia, beginning *b'Tršš* – 'in Tarshish'. The lettering is in archaic style, probably eighth century BC. It has been compared with the earliest known inscription from Carthage (*above*), a gold medallion reading: 'Idamelek, to Ashtart, to Pygmalion . . .'. Pygmalion was probably a local god of Citium in Cyprus. The script appears to be a little later than that of Nora

these early dates is entirely lacking, but evidence of Phoenician activities at a date early in the first millennium has recently been sought in the epigraphy of a stone found *Ill. 115* at Nora, on Cape Pula in southern Sardinia, but there has been considerable disagreement over this, and it is possible that the script is provincial and archaic. If, however, the script is genuinely that of the late ninth century it must be taken as a monument erected by some passing sea-captain rather than as evidence that Phoenician activity was at its height in the island at that date, for nothing so *Ill. 66* early (except possibly the Serra Ilixi ox-hide ingots – mentioned above) shows such early contact. Nevertheless, the stone clearly mentions 'Tarshish', 'Sardinia', and it is tempting to accept it as the monument of some metal prospector in 'Tarshish' in the precolonization period.

The date of 814 claimed by the Sicilian historian Timaeus (who ought to have known) for the foundation of Carthage must be taken into serious consideration. In

117 This pottery from the earliest level of the 'Tanit Precinct' at Carthage, the earliest from the site, is without strict parallel. The cinerary urn (behind) is Cypriot, but the painted ware is of Greek inspiration

spite of the total destruction of the city by the Romans, a considerable amount of material has been recovered from Punic tombs and from a group of votive deposits of children's bones made in a graveyard dedicated to the Carthaginian goddess Tanit. Unfortunately the only datable objects in this material are imported Greek vases in the Proto-Corinthian style, which made their appearance in the west Mediterranean at the earliest at the end of the eighth century. One of these vases was found in a tomb containing an inscription in letters of a style corresponding to that of the Nora Stone in Sardinia. Even a group of pottery with geometric ornament found below the deposits in the Tanit precinct cannot be shown to be earlier than the third quarter of the eighth century. Thus, because of the 'lost century' between the traditional foundation date and the beginning of the archaeological record, many are inclined to place the foundation of Carthage during the period in the late eighth century

Ills. 118, 119

Ill. 117

Ill. 116

when both Greek and Phoenician were active in the west Mediterranean and established themselves in Sicily. The archaeological record of Phoenicians at Motya is almost as early as that of Carthage, whilst evidence for Phoenician establishment in Malta occurs in the early seventh century.

Carthage *seems* to have been 'founded' by Tyre in the period of upheaval following upon the year 700 when the city was solicited on both sides by Esarhaddon and the pharaohs of Dynasty XXV. In 673 BC, Tyre was brought to the critical choice of losing herself to Egypt or making a new foundation overseas. In fact, Tyre was completely overcome by the Assyrians in 666 and reduced to the

118, 119　The bones of children cremated in sacrifice to the goddess Tanit, the Carthaginian Ashtart, were buried in urns in her temple precinct (*Ill. 118* opposite). The urns sometimes had shrines and dedicatory stelae built above them; some of these can be seen in the background. The stratification of the Precinct deposit was valuable in establishing pottery chronology. *Ill. 119* above, shows urns and stelae from 'Tanit II' level, seventh to fourth centuries BC

status of an Assyrian tributary power. Baalu, king of Tyre, escaped with his two daughters Dido and Anna, sailed, and founded Carthage. Dido and Anna we know as the heroines of Virgil's *Aeneid*, which still preserves the tradition of their father's name as Belus (Baalu).

From this must perhaps be separated another tradition mixed with the Dido legend of the foundation of Carthage by Pygmalion, an earlier king of Tyre, and his sister Elissa, whose name probably stems from Alašia, Cyprus. It is possible that this earlier legend applied to the Kartihadesht (Larnaka) already mentioned, which became prominent in the early eighth century.

It seems safe to accept the foundation of Carthage by the second half of the eighth century BC, contemporaneous with or only slightly earlier than the Greek settlement in the west and the foundation of Ischia, Cumae, Syracuse, etc., for it is with these earlier settlements that Carthage shares the same Egyptianizing objects (faience and jewellery in particular) which are found in the earlier grave material.

Recent archaeological work has filled out the picture of Carthaginian expansion in the Mediterranean. Whilst nothing is known of Cadiz, excavated material in Utica, traditionally the oldest foundation, is not older than the seventh century. New sites at Rachgoun, an offshore island near Oran, and Mersa Madakh, on the near-by coast, are apparently of the early sixth century, and work on the Spanish Moroccan sites of Lixus and Tamuda indicates a growth in the communities of that region in the fourth century at which date the rock of Gibraltar was held by Carthaginians, and settlements had been made at Adra and Valencia, for which there is some slight archaeological evidence. After Carthage and Utica, whose high antiquity archaeology has not vindicated, great cities are few. Motya rose to wealth by her proximity to the Sicilo-Greek sphere of trade and doubtless by a mixture of Greek cunning and Phoenician enterprise, but we do

Ill. 120

not know the cause of the prosperity of Sardinian Tharros. Otherwise, a few small towns like Ibiza and Nora and Rusadir (Melilla in Spanish Morocco) were almost certainly primarily concerned with the exploitation of raw materials in their immediate hinterlands. For the rest, we meet but a collection of trading stations and minor ports, mainly established in the fourth century at the earliest, whose miserable architectural remains speak of a very low cultural level. Into this category fall Mersa Madakh, Cap Bon, Sidi Abdselam in Spanish Morocco, Olbia in Sardinia, and various sites on the Levant coast of Spain.

120 Small terracotta masks like this from Tharros (western Sardinia) have been found in many Punic tombs. They appear to be derived from the miniature death-masks known in Phoenicia and Cyprus (*Ill. 111*) but have assumed a grimacing smile, perhaps averting contagion. Sixth century BC

Commerce, for which the sea was a high road rather than a barrier, alone determined the mechanism of this expansion. In no case can any Phoenician penetration of the hinterland for commercial purposes be demonstrated: it was by the provision of markets rather than in exploitation that this commercial empire flourished. The exchanges of Greek and Phoenician merchants in the east Mediterranean, largely by-passing Cyprus, appear to have been particularly significant for the western Phoenicians. Greek traders appear to have operated in Carthage from the beginning, whereas Cypriot exports do not reach the West. Except in Spain and Ibiza, Greeks and Phoenicians seem to have explored the markets together. Motya is an outstanding case, for here Corinthian and Etruscan wares show that the colony was involved in Sicilian Greek trade. Greek traders reached Tharros and Sulcis, and a Greek helmet dredged from the Huelva delta as well as the Phocaean amphorae from Mogador remind us that Ionians in particular were interested in the far west and of the voyage of Kolaios of Samos on a visit to Tartessos, about 630 BC. When Carthage lost the Tartessos market to the Samians, and Spain had become the chief source of silver for the Ionian cities in the sixth century, Carthage was still able to maintain herself by the

121 Shekel of Tyre (obv. and rev.). A dolphin symbolizes her sea dominance; the murex-shell her purple dye industry. The owl, taken from the influential Attic coinage, is Egyptianized. *c.* 450–400 BC

command of the ivory and metals of the North African interior, as well as her own handicrafts in carpentry, cushion-making and fine fabrics and upholstery, to the quality of which ancient authors testify. Exploitation of raw materials such as the pine-pitch and timber of Ibiza and the lead of Sardinian Sulcis as well as the exploitation of the esparto grass of the Valencian coast, and other raw materials of which there is no archaeological record must have provided for the basic economy of the lesser towns. The smaller coastal stations, besides providing the frequent harbourage necessary to a coastal carrying trade, most probably exploited local fisheries as a source of income. Pliny tells us how lagoon fishing with nets slung from stakes set up in shallow water was a particular practice of the Phoenicians and doubtless they introduced present-day lagoon fishing methods to the west Mediterranean. Cagliari, Olbia, Motya are all situated near lagoons, and it is astonishing to see how many Punic settlements (Ibiza, Cadiz, Alcudia de Elche, Sidi Abdselam, Cagliari and Olbia) are situated on the edge of natural salt pans where material was at hand for the preservation of fish. Ibiza, at least, according to Athenaeus, was famous for her kippers, and the large cigar-shaped amphorae with wide mouths found in almost all Punic establishments were doubtless used for the trading of salt or salt-fish. One such amphora was found at Motya full of fish-bones, and offerings of cooked fish were often placed in the tombs where their backbones were still found adhering to the curious little plates with partitions to receive the gravy.

Whether the Phoenicians carried their fishing enterprises into deep waters is difficult to decide. Certainly large fish-hooks and small harpoons have been found in several of the sites, and a number of fish-hooks found with the Punic pottery in Gorham's Cave, Gibraltar,

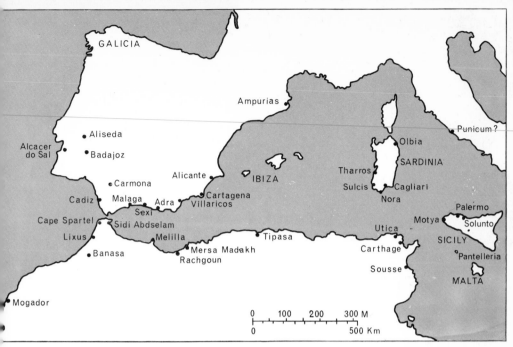

122   Phoenician and Punic colonies and trading stations in the West

leave little doubt as to the occupation of these cave-dwellers. Perhaps the tunny was fished as off the Sardinian west coast in historical times: tunny fish feature on the earliest coinage issued at Cadiz, Rusadir and Cartagena, and a dolphin in combination with the murex purple shell on the earliest issue of Tyre itself.

Ill. 121

Whatever the case, there is no doubt that it was in the middle of the seventh century that Phoenician activity in the west Mediterranean reached its height. Motya, the island city near Marsala in western Sicily, was a flourishing entrepôt between Carthage and Etruria by that date, and by the end of the century Tharros had been founded in the Gulf of Oristano in Sardinia and had trade contact with the people of that island whose resources in bronze and wool were of great value. Both Tharros and Nora have been scientifically excavated recently and shown to be flourishing towns in the sixth–fifth centuries B C. After the earlier discovery at Nora of a precinct for

Ill. 122

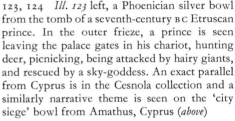

123, 124 *Ill. 123* left, a Phoenician silver bowl from the tomb of a seventh-century BC Etruscan prince. In the outer frieze, a prince is seen leaving the palace gates in his chariot, hunting deer, picnicking, being attacked by hairy giants, and rescued by a sky-goddess. An exact parallel from Cyprus is in the Cesnola collection and a similarly narrative theme is seen on the 'city siege' bowl from Amathus, Cyprus (*above*)

125 The Phoenician toiletry industry exported marble scent-bottles such as this from Vulci, Etruria. Late seventh century BC

cremated offerings similar to the precinct of Tanit now comes the find of an earlier group of deposits at Sulcis (S. Antioco) datable, like that on Motya, to about 700–600 BC. A settlement on the Balearic island of Ibiza was also made, according to the traditional date, in the middle of this century, although no material earlier than the fifth century has yet been found on the island. Trade between Ibiza and the near-by Greek colony of Emporion (Ampurias) was brisk and, apart from the importance of the raw materials of Ibiza, it was probably in rivalry to the 'Greek corner' of the north-western Mediterranean that Ibiza found her role.

It cannot be said that the civilization of the western Mediterranean owes much artistically to the foundation of these colonies. The second quarter of the seventh century was the hey-day of Orientalizing trade in Etruria to which date must be assigned the gilded silver vessels with Phoenician design found in the rich tomb of Cerveteri and Praeneste (Palestrina) and small faience

126, 127 Probably illustrating a lost myth, the outer frieze of this Phoenician bowl from Idalium (Cyprus) depicts the 'labours' of a pair of gods – perhaps Melqart and the prototype of Greek Herakles. A Phoenician bowl from Italy (*right*), depicts Phoenician maidens in a ritual dance. Both mid-seventh century B C

juglets in human shape and amulets probably made by Phoenicians resident in Rhodes. The bowls appear to be either of Cypriot origin or to be copies of Cypriot work made by Etruscan artists. The use of the Madonna lily as a marker on some of these bowls is a particularly Cypriot device and a bowl from the Bernardini tomb has a very close parallel from Amathus. Both Phoenicians and Ionian Greeks had a hand in this trade in objects from the east. The presence in earlier contexts of Urartian metalwork and copies of Cretan work, the former of which probably reached Greece and Etruria alike from some Ionian source, suggests that there were channels for the dispersal of Orientalizing objects other than those opened by the Phoenicians. At any rate, none of these pieces of Phoenician or Urartian metalwork appears to have reached Carthage. The wealth of the Phoenician metalwork in Etruscan tombs (bowls, jugs, and small pieces of jewellery) is almost certainly due to the establishment of a Phoenician workshop making objects for the local market

Ill. 125

Ills. 126, 127

Ill. 123
Ill. 124

128 Phoenician motifs on a granulated gold belt, Aliseda (Cáceres, Spain). The 'Aliseda treasure' also contained a glass jug with an Egyptian hieroglyphic inscription, now paralleled on alabaster jars recently excavated at Almuñecar, ancient Sexi

from the local sources of Italian silver. Gold and silver objects of Ionian and local styles were produced by these shops whose influence upon native arts was very great. Their position was, as we shall see, paralleled in Iberian Spain but, for some unknown reason, not in Carthagian North Africa.

Tarshish–Tartessos

The name of another land to which Hiram and Solomon sent trading expeditions was Tarshish: its name is linked with Ophir as denoting the most distant lands of Biblical trade. The specially large freighters constructed to make these long-distance voyages were known as 'ships of Tarshish', thus leading to some confusion regarding the locality of this mysterious place, since ships of Tarshish also sailed to Ophir. The post-Solomonic Biblical authors had only the vaguest idea where Tarshish was – it became a Timbuktu of antiquity – and they confused the cargoes

129 'Tartessian' goldwork discovered at El Carambolo (Seville). The cluster of seals mounted on a necklace (centre) is certainly Phoenician, as is the inspiration of other goldwork found at Sanlúcar (Evora) at the Guadalquivir mouth. Iberian influence is seen in the shape of the 'spacer' (lower centre). Seventh century BC

from these distant lands in general exoticism – gold, silver, ivory, apes and peacocks. Traditionally Tarshish has been connected with the realm of Tartessos in southern Spain, known principally from the sixth-century Greek logbook *Ora Maritima* of Festus Avienus, and thought to have been on the Huelva or Guadalquivir estuaries. The names of its kings are known, the most famous of which was Arganthonios who died about 550 BC. The gold, silver, copper and tin of this region were certainly exploited by prehistoric peoples, but no evidence of Phoenician presence in the region early in the first millennium has been unearthed. The rich treasure of goldwork found at Aliseda, Cáceres, and recent finds of golden jewellery at Seville and Evora, whilst both markedly Iberian in aspects of style, bear a strong influence of Phoenician jewellery techniques. Neither of these 'Tartessian' treasures, however, can be shown to date earlier than the eighth century, whilst that of Aliseda

Ill. 128

Ill. 129

130 Bone comb from tumulus burials at Carmona (Guadalquivir valley). The griffin is Oriental but with Greek-type wings, whilst the lion and goats may be of local inspiration: no precise parallel to this art style is known. Other ivories from Carmona have stylistic parallels in seventh century B C Carthage

Ills. 130, 131
Ill. 132

probably belongs to the second half of the seventh. Of similar date are the Carthaginian-style ivories from Celtic tumuli at Carmona near Seville and a number of bronze and silver jugs of 'Samaria ware' shape found at Carmona, Badajoz and elsewhere. These jugs and jewellery techniques are paralleled in contemporary Etruria, and it is probable that the name Tarshish referred in Solomonic times to the west Mediterranean mining areas in general, and more particularly to the metal-bearing areas of Tuscany, Sardinia and Spain. Also, independently of the foundation of Carthage, Phoenician craftsmen of later times in the seventh century B C renewed these contacts and established jewellers' shops for the local markets amongst the Iberians and Etruscans, with a particularly flourishing one at Tartessos. The equation Tarshish–Tartessos is therefore only partially correct and without strict philological basis, but the references to Tarshish in Assyrian inscriptions certainly imply that it was at the opposite end of the Mediterranean from Cyprus. At the same time it is becoming increasingly clear from archaeological finds that there existed in southern Spain some vigorous Phoenician centre independent of Carthage which has yet to be discovered.

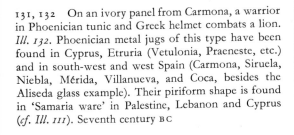

131, 132   On an ivory panel from Carmona, a warrior
in Phoenician tunic and Greek helmet combats a lion.
Ill. 132. Phoenician metal jugs of this type have been
found in Cyprus, Etruria (Vetulonia, Praeneste, etc.)
and in south-west and west Spain (Carmona, Siruela,
Niebla, Mérida, Villanueva, and Coca, besides the
Aliseda glass example). Their piriform shape is found
in 'Samaria ware' in Palestine, Lebanon and Cyprus
(*cf. Ill. 111*). Seventh century BC

Beyond the Pillars of Hercules

Ancient authorities are agreed that the Atlantic was a
Phoenician preserve. Punic ships passed Gibraltar and
plied along the Atlantic coasts gaining access to Tartessos
and the unlocated 'Tin Isles' or Kassiterides, possibly
Galicia. From the distribution of recognizably Punic finds
in Portugal and western Spain it appears that their craft
sailed the navigable rivers, the Guadiana and the Tagus,
trading with the Lusitanian Celtic tribes. The most important tumuli at Carmona are on the Guadalquivir, and it
appears trade was radiating from the south-west by the
main river valleys and not from the Levantine coast of
Spain. In Portugal, besides a few pieces of jewellery showing Phoenician inspiration, Punic pottery from the Celtic
oppidum at Santa Olaya at the mouth of the Mondego
shows that trade was carried on there, whilst at Alcacer
do Sal to the south pottery from some ill-documented
graves suggests that these were Phoenician burials of the

seventh century. It cannot be shown with certainty that Phoenician traders ventured farther north, let alone to Britain, but the wealth of glass beads of Punic types and an occasional ornament from the Galician castra suggests that they had some contact with the farthest tip of Spain.

Ships leaving the roadsteads of Lixus and Tangier made for the island port of Mogador, some six hundred miles south of the Pillars of Hercules, off the coast of French Morocco. Pottery from the lowest stratified deposit of Mogador island is certainly of the earlier part of the sixth century B C and contains pieces of Cypriot and Phocaean Greek wares. It is possible that this is the station of 'Karikon Teichos' visited by the Carthagian general Hanno who was commissioned to explore the West African coast in *c.* 500 B C, doubtless in an attempt to reach Senegal or Gabon. Much of the Mogador pottery belongs to a sub-group of Punic wares (characterized by a brilliantly burnished red-slip) apparently confined to Spain and the far west of North Africa. Other Mogador vessels, however, link closely with high-collared urns from Carmona, Rachgoun, Alcacer do Sal and Valencia. Most likely in these non-typical relatives of Punic pottery we may recognize the pottery of lost Tartessos.

How did the Phoenicians of the narrow coastal strip of Lebanon and Palestine with their poor resources, political disunity and restricted man-power manage to settle this network of small communities? The genius of the Carthaginians, like that of the Tyrians in Cyprus, consisted in planting but a small number of colonials and allowing them to mix freely with the local populations. To the Greeks these bastard communities were known as the Libyphoenices of Africa, and the Bastulophoenices of south-eastern Spain.

CHAPTER SIX

Conclusions

It is difficult to assess the part of the Levant in the history
of material civilization, in which it played the role of
transmitter rather than that of originator. The Canaanite
role in literary history, however, is now beginning to be
realized. Long after Sidon had been destroyed by Esarhaddon in 675 and Ashurbanipal had finally come down
upon Tyre 'like the wolf on the fold' in 666 and extin-
guished her last breath, names such as Zeno, the philo-
sopher-founder of Stoicism (333–261 BC), born in Citium,
and the philosophers Boethus of Sidon and Antipater of
Tyre, though all belonged to strongly Hellenized communities, were still regarded by the Greeks as continuing
the Phoenician tradition of acumen. Philo of Byblos (first
century AD) in the composition of his work on Phoenician
religion claimed as his authority an eleventh-century
Phoenician priest-historian Sanchuniathon of Berytus.
The existence of this Phoenician source has long been
disputed, but correspondences between his statements
and the fresh mythological documents found at Ugarit are
striking and leave little doubt of his authenticity.

The recovery of Ugaritic literature has been one of the
major archaeological advances made this century and has
added new dimensions to our understanding of the
ancient Near East. The epics reflect the mixed religious

stratification of the city – Semitic, Hurrian and Hittite – and besides throwing valuable light on Biblical thinking, ritual and phraseology, provide a prototype for the epic tradition of Greek literature. Some of the material is of a ritual kind connected with that promotion of seasonal fertility so vital to a gardening and farming community. The theme of the dying and rising god is here told more fully than elsewhere in the Near East: Mot, the spirit of death, banishes Baal, the lord of vegetation, as is appropriate in a land where summer drought puts an end to vegetation, but with the renewal of the rain in autumn Baal renews his victory over Mot and in a divine marriage with Anath, the fertility goddess, fecundates the earth. Such tales, told in elaborate detail and intended certainly for recitation if not dramatic acting, contain the germ of Greek drama. The Ugaritic interest in romantic themes, jealousies and rivalries amongst the gods, as well as in feasting and violence, all generally foreign to the literatures of Babylonia and Egypt, is part of a heroic literary tradition which was perhaps widespread in the Late Bronze Age Levant. Claims of indirect thematic connections between the Ugaritic and Homeric poems have little foundation. Whilst the theme of the warlike expedition for the winning and recovery of a beautiful bride is found both in the Ugaritic Epic of King Keret and in the *Iliad* story of Helen of Troy, the circumstances of both tales are entirely different. Many of the literary 'borrowings' of Hesiod and Homer seem to have been made from Anatolian literature rather than from Ugarit, and such parallels as occur are more likely due to the undeniable Hurrian element in Ugaritic saga. Nevertheless the world of Homer had much in common with that of Ugarit – generations of mountain-dwelling gods, a benign father god, an Hephaistos-like god of craftsmanship, and some others. Explanations of these parallels by transmission through lost literatures are tempting but not

133 Whilst Baal, Reshef and the goddesses are frequently represented in Canaanite art, images of El, the benign father, are rare. A carved block and this painted tankard from Ras Shamra, both depicting a bearded god seated at a banquet, may be taken to represent him (*c.* 1300 BC)

compelling. Philistine literature might indeed have formed a three-way path between Ugaritic, Biblical and Aegean literatures, for it seems likely that the mercenaries of the 'Caphtorian' Philistines exerted an artistic influence in the artistic court of King David, but so far we lack proof that they had an oral poetic tradition let alone written literature. The claim that the users of Linear A script from the court centres of east Minoan Crete were 'Phoenician' Semitic colonists is not sufficiently substantiated to allow us to suppose that Ugaritic and other Near Eastern epic material survived in Eteocretan literature, though there seems to have been an undeniable link between Crete and Ugarit at the time the epics were composed.

The Canaanite legacy to the Hebrew is more tangible and is closely demonstrable in the structure and phraseology of Psalms (*e.g.* 88, 89) but, above all, the very Hebrew idea of Jahweh as the father and creator of mankind seems to have been adopted from the Ugaritic idea of El, the benign father of the Ugaritic pantheon.

Yet a great gulf separates the literature of Canaan on the one hand and that of the Greeks and Hebrews on the other.

Although the Ugaritic stories imply the observance of social obligations, these are never raised by philosophic reflection to the level of morally binding obligations. They were preoccupied with ritual and symbolic situations, and hence with only idealized relationships in personal and political matters. Nowhere do they deal with personal actions morally judged by an accepted code; and nowhere are the symbolical actions applied personally: the Canaanites did not for instance apply the theory of the dying and rising god to a personal ideology as did the Greeks from the similar cult of Adonis, or the Egyptians from the mystery cult of Osiris.

The Ugaritic poems accept the world as ready-made, do not moralize upon its significance, or preoccupy themselves with theology or ethics or conceptions of life after death. Notions of that humanism which magnifies the literature of Greece and the Bible and had already on a small scale been attempted by Sumerian proverbs and wisdom literature were absent. For its essentially amoral character the Hebrews condemned it.

Writing

It now appears that the distinctive and highly successful systems evolved in Egypt (hieroglyphs) and Mesopotamia (cuneiform) were not the only attempts at pre-alphabetic writing in the ancient Near East. In the Aegean, Linear B appears to have been in use from about 1350 BC, and before this the Linear A syllabary, held by certain scholars to be the script of a Semitic language, was in use at Knossos, Kato Zakro and other palaces in Crete. Cypro-Minoan was, as we have seen an Aegean-type linear

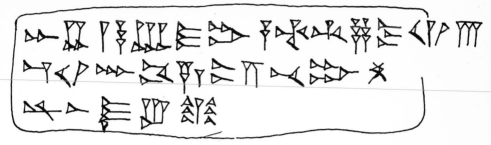

134 Clay tablet from Ras Shamra: the oldest known ABC, setting out the 27 main consonants and 3 vowel signs of the Ugaritic cuneiform alphabet. Fourteenth century BC

system, certainly syllabic; and two independent systems of writing on some tablets from Byblos (*c.* 1600 BC) and Tell Deir Alla in the Jordan valley (Late Bronze Age – discovered in 1963), whilst undeciphered, appear to be syllabic. All these are, however, minor systems compared with the general usage or currency of Akkadian cuneiform script which was found acceptable for the occasional transcription of non-Semitic languages. It is not surprising therefore that the earliest consistent attempt at *alphabetic* writing, that of the Ugaritic of the Ras Shamra documents, took its letter-forms from cuneiform script. Outside Ras Shamra, written Ugaritic has been found only at near-by Tell Sukas, but two examples have now come to light in southern Palestine of an alphabetic cuneiform script different from that in use at Ugarit. A twelfth-century clay tablet from Canaanite Taanach in the plain

Ill. 134

Ill. 135

135 Clay tablet with alphabetic cuneiform from Tell Taanach in the Esdraeldon plain: 'From Kokaba, belonging to P–.8 *kprt* measures of sifted flour'. Twelfth to thirteenth centuries BC

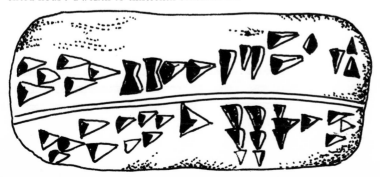

of Esdraeldon appears to be a receipt for a delivery of flour, whilst a tablet of the fourteenth century from Beth Shemesh appears to carry a prayer to the Canaanite goddess of birth to produce pregnancy. These tablets suggest that there were several experiments with cuneiform alphabets as indeed with the letter-forms of the linear alphabet which eventually dominated.

Ill. 136

The invention of a linear alphabet by the Canaanites was the last stage of a long process of evolution beginning with what does not merit the name of writing, but was merely pictography. Mesopotamian peoples developed such a system and also invented a phonetic system in which signs stand for various syllables; it was in this way that the cuneiform languages of Mesopotamia were written. Egyptian hieroglyphic writing developed in a similar manner, but went further by its use of what is called acrophony, or the restriction of phonetic value of certain signs to their initial consonants only. This produced a kind of alphabetic writing first employed in the second millennium amongst the Semitic workers in the Egyptian turquoise mines at Serabit el-Khadem in the Sinai peninsula. These Sinaitic inscriptions (formerly dated about 2000 but now believed to be considerably later) employ signs derived from Egyptian hieroglyphs and others which do not belong to any Egyptian system of writing. Some of the non-Egyptian signs relate to the earliest known alphabetic inscription from Phoenicia written in the tenth century on the stone coffin of Ahiram, king of Byblos.

Ill. 137
Ill. 138

Before this date, however, writing more removed from Egyptian hieroglyphs is found painted on potsherds in the area of southern Palestine: at Shechem, Gaza and Lachish. These are obviously alphabetic, although their interpretation is controversial, and upon archaeological evidence they date from slightly before 1500 BC. The discovery of inscribed javelin heads dating from about

Ill. 139

SINAITIC SCRIPT	DISCRIPTION OF SIGN	CANAANITE SCRIPT OF 13 th. CENT. B.C.	CANAANITE SCRIPT OF C. 1000 B.C.	SOUTH ARAB SCRIPT OF IRON AGE	MODERN HEBREW SCRIPT	PHONTIC VALUE
	OX - HEAD					ʾ
	HOUSE					b
?						g̱
	FISH					d
	MAN PRAYING					h
?						w
?						z
	?					ḏ
	FENCE					ḥ
	DOUBLE - LOOP					ḫ
?						ṭ
?						y
	PALM OF HAND					k
	"OX - GOAD"					l
	WATER					m
	SERPENT					n
?						s
	EYE					ʿ
?						ḡ
	THROW STICK					p
?						ṣ
	BLOSSOM					ḍ ẓ
	?					q
	HUMAN HEAD					r
	BOW					ṯ ś
	?					š
	MARK OF CROSS					t

136   The development of the alphabetic linear Semitic scripts. Archaic Greek scripts derived forms from the Canaanite in column 4

137, 138 The inscription of the sarcophagus of Ahiram, King of Byblos, is the longest piece of early Phoenician script. It was executed in the eleventh century BC on the lid of an earlier sarcophagus and overlay an inscription in Byblian 'pseudo-hieroglyphic' script still traceable. The reliefs on the sarcophagus itself (*opposite*), show a funerary meal and mourners. The figures on the lid are in thirteenth-century style

the eleventh century, and also of more late-thirteenth-century inscribed words, makes it now easier to fill in the general lines of evolution of this Proto-Canaanite script from the sixteenth to tenth centuries. One of the remarkable features of this evolution is that between the fifteenth and thirteenth centuries the change from vertical to horizontal script turns the signs ninety degrees so that the finished product, whilst looking more like the letters of the Phoenician alphabet of the first millennium, look less like Egyptian hieroglyphs.

It is not known from which Phoenician centre the Greeks learned the alphabet, but a theoretical claim can be made for Al Mina where Greeks and Phoenicians were intimate. Certainly the Euboean Greeks who founded Al Mina preserved a very archaic alphabet, although it cannot be shown that they used it as early as other Greek islands. Another factor pointing perhaps to Al Mina is the adoption by the Phrygians, as instanced in the inscriptions from Gordium, of a Phoenician-derived alphabet as early as any archaic Greek script. The lack of consistency in the direction of which the Greeks wrote gives to early Greek writing a great variety of forms, but archaic inscriptions from Thera and Rhodes, for instance, have forms tolerably close to those of the Ahiram sarcophagus. The date at which the Greeks began alphabetic writing was probably in the early eighth century BC, but there is

between this date and surviving examples a gap in which many variations had already taken place. Thus we cannot tell whether there was originally a number of personally derived alphabets or whether there was one general alphabet altered by the vicissitudes of transmission. By the end of that century such inscribed late geometric Greek vases as have now been found in the graves of the early Euboean settlers on Ischia near Naples transmitted alphabetic forms to Italy.

Although the alphabet is the greatest of Levantine legacies, we are now beginning to realize the cultural and religious debt which ancient Greece, and hence we ourselves, owe to the ancient Levantine world. Further discoveries will surely reveal a cultural continuity between the ancient Levant and archaic Greece which was hitherto unsuspected. Meanwhile let us summarize the character of ancient Levantine civilization under one of its most cherished symbols, *malum punicum*, the pomegranate which

139 Bronze dagger with incised signs from a tomb at Tell ed-Duweir (Lachish), 1700–1600 BC. The signs belong to an early stage of the emergence of alphabetic script in Palestine, but except for the head, which represents the Semitic *resh* 'r', the reading is uncertain

the Phoenicians planted throughout the Mediterranean. Luscious but hard of skin, wholesome but fragmentary, vivid but shallow, seedy but ever-refreshing, ripe but enduring, and if not the most palatable, at least the most shapely fruit.

Bibliography

List of Illustrations

Index

Bibliography

Abbreviations

AJA   *American Journal of Archaeology*
BA   *Biblical Archaeologist*
BASOR   *Bulletin of the American Schools of Oriental Research*
Goldman, 1956   *The Aegean and the Near East; Essays presented to H. Goldman,* edited by
     S. Weinberg. New York, 1956
IEJ   *Israel Exploration Journal*
ILN   *Illustrated London News*
JNES   *Journal of Near Eastern Studies*
JSS   *Journal of Semitic Studies*
RB   *Revue Biblique*

Travels and Voyages

BARNETT, R. D. Early Shipping in the Near East, *Antiquity*, 32, 1958, pp. 220–30
CASSON, L. *The Ancient Mariners: Seafarers and Sea-fighters of the Mediterranean in Ancient Times.*
     London, 1959
GLUECK, N. The Topography and History of Ezion-Geber and Elath, *BASOR*, 72, 1938,
     pp. 2–13
HENNIG, W. *Terrae Incognitae, Vol. I.* Leiden, 1936
VAN BEEK, G. W. Frankincense and Myrrh, *BA*, XXIII, 3, 1960, pp. 70–95

Early History and Chronology

ALBRIGHT, W. F. The Eighteenth Century Princes of Byblos and the Chronology of the Middle
     Bronze Age, *BASOR*, 176, 1964, pp. 38–46
BRAIDWOOD, R. *Excavations in the Plain of Antioch I.* Chicago, 1960
CONTENSON, H. DE. New Correlations Between Ras Shamra and al-Amuq, *BASOR*, 172, 1965,
     pp. 35–40
GELB, I. J. The Early History of the West Semitic Peoples, *Journal of Cuneiform Studies*, 15, 1961,
     pp. 27–47
GOETZE, A. *Hethiter, Churriter und Assyrer.* Oslo, 1936
HAYES, W. C., *et al. Chronology: Egypt, Western Asia and the Aegean Bronze Age*, Cambridge
     Ancient History, fasc. 4, 1962
KUPPER, J. R. *Northern Mesopotamia and Syria*, Cambridge Ancient History, fasc. 14, 1963
SCHAEFFER, C. F. A. *Stratigraphie et chronologie comparée de l'Asie occidentale.* Oxford, 1948
SMITH, S. *Alalakh and Chronology.* London, 1940
WOOLLEY, C. L. *Alalakh: an account of Excavations at Tell Atchana in the Hatay, 1937–49.* Oxford,
     1955

The Sargonid Period

FALKNER, M. Studien zur Geographie des Alten Mesopotamien, *Archiv für Orientforschung*,
     18, 1957–8, pp. 1–37
GADD, C. J. *The Dynasty of Agade and the Gutian Invasion.* Cambridge Ancient History, fasc. 15,
     1963
— Seals of Ancient Indian Style found at Ur. *Proceedings, British Academy*, 18, 1932, p. 191

OPPENHEIM, A. L. The Seafaring Merchants of Ur, *Journal of the American Oriental Society*, 74, 1954, pp. 6–17
WEIDNER, E. F. Das Reich von Akkad, *Archiv für Orientforschung*, 16, 1952–3, pp. 1–15

Byblos

DUNAND, M. *Fouilles de Byblos*, 2 vols. Paris, 1937, 19, 39
MONTET, P. *Byblos et l'Egypte*, 2 vols. Paris, 1928

Mari and Syrian Trade

DAVIES, N. DE G. and FAULKNER, R. O. A Syrian trading venture to Egypt, *Jour. Egyptian Arch.*, 33, 1947, pp. 40–6
DOSSIN, G. Les archives économiques du Palais de Mari, *Syria*, XXXII, 1955, pp. 1–8
LEEMANS, W. F. *Foreign Trade in the Old Babylonian Period*. Leiden, 1960
PARROT, A. *Mission archeologue de Mari: II. Le Palais*. 3 vols. Paris, 1958, 1959
— *Le Temple d'Ishtar*. Paris, 1956, 1958
PARROT, A. and DOSSIN, G. *Archives royales de Mari, I–XV*. Paris, 1950–4
TOCCI, F. M. *La Siria nell'età di Mari*. Rome, 1960

Hurrians—Mitanni

GELB, I. J. *Hurrians and Subarians*. Chicago, 1944
HROUDA, B. Die Churriter als Problem der archäologischen Forschung, *Archaeologia Geographica*, 7, 1958, pp. 14–19
O'CALLAGHAN, R. T. *Aram Naharaim*. Rome, 1948
SPEISER, E. A. The Hurrian Participation in the Civilizations of Mesopotamia, Syria and Palestine, *Cahiers d'histoire mondiale*, 1, 2, 1953, pp. 311–27

Ras Shamra

DUSSAUD, R. *Les découvertes de Ras Shamra (Ugarit) et l'Ancien Testament*. 2nd ed. Paris, 1941
LIVERANI, M. *Storia di Ugarit nell'età degli archivi politici*. Rome, 1962
RAINEY, A. F. Foreign Business Agents at Ugarit, *IEJ*, 13, 4, 1963, pp. 313–21
SCHAEFFER, C. F. A. *Ugaritica, I–IV*. Paris, 1939–62
SCHAEFFER, C. F. A. and NOUGAYROL, J. *Le Palais royal d'Ugarit; Mission de Ras Shamra*, vols. VI, VII, IX. Paris, 1955–7

Syro-Canaanite Art

BOSSERT, H. *Altsyrien*. Tübingen, 1951
FRANKFORT, H. *Art and Architecture of the Ancient Orient*. Rev. ed. London, 1958
KANTOR, H. J. Syro-Palestinian Ivories, *JNES*, XV, 1956, pp. 153–74
MATTHIAE, P. *Ars Syra; contributi alla storia dell'arte figurativa siriana etc*. Rome, 1962

Canaanite Literature

AISTLEITNER, J. *Die Mythologischen und Kultischen Texte aus Ras Schamra*. 2nd ed. Budapest, 1964
DRIVER, G. R. *Canaanite Myths and Legends*. Edinburgh, 1956
GASTER, T. *Thespis*. New York, 1961
GORDON, C. H. *Ugaritic Literature*. Rome, 1949
GRAY, J. *The Legacy of Canaan*, Vetus Testamentum Suppl. V. Leiden, 1957
— *The Krt Text in the Literature of Ras Shamra; A Social Myth of Ancient Canaan*. 2nd ed. Leiden, 1964
KAPELRUD, A. S. *Baal in the Ras Shamra Texts*. Copenhagen, 1952
POPE, M. H. *El in the Ugaritic Texts*. Leiden, 1955

Mycenaean Relations with Egypt and the Levant

ASTOUR, M. C. *Hellenosemitica; An ethnic and cultural study in West Semitic impact on Mycenaean Greece.* Leiden, 1965

CATLING, H. W. and KARAGEORGHIS, V. Minoika in Cyprus, *Annual of the British School at Athens,* 55, 1960, pp. 109–27

DESBOROUGH, V. R. d'A. *The Last Mycenaeans and their Successors, An Archaeological Survey,* c. 1200–1000 BC. Oxford, 1964

GRACE, V. The Canaanite Jar, *Goldman,* 1956

KANTOR, H. J. *The Aegean and the Orient in the Second Millennium BC.* Archaeological Institute of America Monographs, I, IV, 1947

PENDLEBURY, J. *Aegyptiaca; Catalogue of Egyptian Objects in the Aegean Area.* Cambridge, 1930

STUBBINGS, L. *Mycenaean Pottery from the Levant.* Cambridge, 1951

VERCOUTTER, J. *L'Egypte et le monde préhellénique; étude critique des sources égyptiennes.* Institut français d'archéologie orientale, Cairo, 1956

Late Bronze Age Cyprus

CATLING, H. *Cypriot Bronze Work in the Mycenaean World.* Oxford, 1964

SCHAEFFER, C. F. A. *Enkomi-Alasia.* Paris, 1952

SJÖQVIST, E. *Problems of the Late Cypriot Bronze Age.* Stockholm, 1940

Palestinian Bronze and Iron Ages

AHARONI, Y. and AMIRAM, R. A New Scheme for the Sub-division of the Iron Age in Palestine, *IEJ,* 8, 3, 1958, pp. 171–84

ALBRIGHT, W. F. *The Archaeology of Palestine.* 2nd ed. London, 1960

ALT, A. *Die Herkunft der Hyksos in neuer Sicht.* Sächsische Akademied. Wissenschaften Berichte, 101. Leipzig, 1954

ANATI, E. *Palestine Before the Hebrews.* London, 1963

ENGBERG, R. M. *The Hyksos Reconsidered.* Chicago, 1939

KENYON, K. M. *Archaeology in the Holy Land.* 2nd ed. London, 1964

MALAMAT, A. The Kingdom of David and Solomon in its Contact with Aram Naharaim, *BA,* XXI, 4, 1958, pp. 96–102

MAY, H. G. *Material Remains of the Megiddo Cult.* Chicago, 1935

TUFFNELL, O. *Lachish II: the Fosse Temple.* Oxford, 1940

— *Lachish III: The Iron Age.* Oxford, 1953

— *Lachish IV: The Bronze Age.* Oxford, 1957

YADIN, Y. *Hazor I, II.* Jerusalem, 1953, 1960

Semitic Peoples, General

GIBSON, J. C. Light from Mari on the Patriarchs, *JSS,* VII, 1, 1962, pp. 44–62

GRAY, J. *The Canaanites.* London, 1964

HARDEN, D. B. *The Phoenicians.* London, 1962

MEEK, T. J. *Hebrew Origins.* New York, 1960

MOSCATI, S. *Ancient Semitic Civilizations.* London, 1957.

Phoenicia and the Philistine Region

DOTHAN, T. Archaeological Reflections on the Philistine Problem, *Antiquity and Survival,* II, 2–3, 1957, pp. 151–64

JENSEN, L. B. Royal Purple of Tyre, *JNES,* XII, 2, 1963, pp. 104–18

HITTI, P. *A History of Lebanon.* London, 1957

NOTH, M. Zum Ursprung der phönikischen Küstenstädte, *Welt des Orients*, 47, 1951, pp. 21–8
WRIGHT, G. E. Philistine Coffins and Mercenaries, *BA*, XXII, 1959, pp. 54–66

Iron Age Cyprus

BIRMINGHAM, J. Chronology of Some Early and Middle Iron Age Cypriot Sites, *AJA*, 67, 1963, pp. 15–42
GJERSTAD, E., *et al. Swedish Cyprus Expedition; Finds and Results of the Excavations in Cyprus 1927–1931*. 2 vols. Stockholm, 1934, 1935

Phoenician Art

BARNETT, R. D. *A Catalogue of the Nimrud Ivories*. London, 1957
DESCHAMPS DE MERTZENFELD, C. *Inventaire commenté des ivoires phéniciens*. Paris, 1954
MALLOWAN, M. E. L. *Nimrud and its remains*. 2 vols. London, 1966
STUCCI, S. Un Nuovo Fragmento di Tridacna Incisa, *Bollettino d'arte*, 44, 1959, pp. 158–66

Orientalizing Art

BARNETT, R. D. Oriental Influence on Archaic Greece, *Goldman*, 1956
BLOCH, R. *Etruscan Art*. London, 1959
BROCK, J. K. *Fortetsa: Early Greek Tombs Near Knossos*. Cambridge, 1957
DUNBABIN, T. J. *The Greeks and their Eastern Neighbours*. London, 1957
KUNZE, E. *Kretische Bronzereliefs*. Stuttgart, 1931
MÜHLESTEIN, H. *Die Kunst der Etrusker*. Berlin, 1929
PARETI, L. *La Tomba Regolini—Galassi*. Vatican City, 1947

Aramaean and Syro-Hittite States

AKURGAL, E. *The Art of the Hittites*. London, 1962
BOSSERT, H. Die phönizisch-hethitischen Bilinguen von Karatepe, *Oriens*, I, pp. 163–92; II, pp. 72–120
LANDSBERGER, B. *Sam'al; Studien zur Entdeckung der Ruinenstädte Karatepe*, I. Ankara, 1948
MAZAR, B. The Aramaean Empire and Its Relations with Israel, *BA*, XXV, 4, 1962, pp. 98–120
WOOLLEY, SIR L. and BARNETT, R. D. *Carchemish, Part III*. London, 1952

The Greeks in the East

ALBRIGHT, W. F. Northeast-Mediterranean Dark Ages, *Goldman*, 1956
BOARDMAN, J. *The Greeks Overseas*. Harmondsworth, 1964
RIIS, J. L'activité de la mission archéologique danoise sur la côte phénicienne, *Les Annales Archéologiques de Syrie*, VIII–IX, 1954–59; X, 1960

The Western Phoenicians

ALBRIGHT, W. F. New Light on the Early History of Phoenician Colonization, *BASOR*, 83, 1964, pp. 14–22
BLANCO, FREIJEIRO, A. Orientalia, *Archivo Español de Arqueologia*, XXXIII, 1960, pp. 3–43
CIASCA, A. *et al. Mozia I*. Rome, 1965
CINTAS, P. *Céramique Punique*. Paris, 1950
— *Contribution à l'étude de l'expansion carthaginoise au Maroc*. Paris, 1954
GARCIA Y BELLIDO, A. *Fenicios y Cartagineses en Occidente*. Madrid, 1942
PICARD, G. and C. *Everyday Life in Carthage*. London, 1961
WARMINGTON, B. H. *Carthage*. Harmondsworth, 1964.

Homer and Ugaritic Literature

DIRLMEIER, F. Homerisches Epos und Orient, *Rheinisches Museum für Philologie*, 98, 1955, pp. 18–37

GORDON, C. *Before the Bible*. London, 1962

Development of the Alphabet

ALBRIGHT, W. F. The Early Alphatic Inscriptions from Sinai and their Decipherment, *BASOR*, 110, 1948, pp. 6–20

CROSS, F. M. The Evolution of the Proto-Canaanite Alphabet, *BASOR*, 134, 1954, pp. 15–25

CROSS, F. M. and MILIK, J. T. Inscribed Javelin Heads of the Period of the Judges, etc. *BASOR*, 134, 1954, pp. 5–15

DIRINGER, D. *The Alphabet: A Key to the History of Mankind*. London, 1947

— *Writing*. London, 1962

DRIVER, G. R. *Semitic Writing from Pictograph to Alphabet*. London, 1954

JEFFREYS, L. H. *The Local Scripts of Archaic Greece, etc.* Oxford, 1961

SOBELMAN, F. The Proto-Byblian Inscriptions: A Fresh Approach, *JSS*, VI, 2, 1961, pp. 226–45

VAN DEN BRANDEN, A. Essai de déchiffrement des inscriptions de Deir 'Alla, *Vetus Testamentum*, XV, 2, 1965, pp. 129–50

Short General Reports of Recent Excavations

ACHZIB (Achzhiv, Israel) Phoenician Tombs: M. Prausnitz, *RB*, 69, 3, 1962, pp. 404–5

ASHDOD (Israel) Philistine and later Iron Age levels: M. Dothan, *IEJ*, 13, 4, 1963, pp. 340–2

AZOR (Israel) Philistine and Phoenician burials: M. Dothan, *IEJ*, 11, 4, 1961, pp. 171–5

DEIR 'ALLA (Jordan) Late Bronze Age levels and inscribed tablets: H. Franken, *Vetus Testamentum*, XIV, 1964, pp. 415–22; *ILN*, April 17 and May 1, 1965

EIN GEV (Israel) Iron Age Levels; B. Mazar *et al.*, *IEJ*, 14, 1, 1964, pp. 1–33

KAFR MONASH (Israel) Hoard of Early Bronze Age Tools: R. Hestrin and M. Tadmor, *IEJ*, 13, 4, 1963, pp. 265–88

KATO ZAKRO (Crete) Rich finds from Minoan Palace: N. Platon, *ILN*, March 4, 1964

LARNAKA (Citium, Cyprus) Mycenaean settlement: V. Karageorghis, *ILN*, Dec. 22, 1962; *Bulletin de Correspondance hellénique*, 1961–3

MOGADOR (Morocco) Punic settlement: A. Jodin, Note préliminaire sur l'établissement pré-romain de Mogador, *Bull. d'arch. Marocaine*, II, 1957, pp. 10–40

MOTYA (Mozia, Sicily) Phoenician remains: B. Isserlin, *ILN*, March 3, 1962; Sept. 21, 1963

MOUNT SIRAI (Sardinia) Punic shrine: S. Moscati, *ILN*, April 3, 1965

NAHAL MISHMAR (Israel) Early Bronze Age copper hoard from the 'Cave of Treasure': *IEJ*, 12, 3–4, 1962, pp. 215–26; P. Bar-Adon, *Archaeology*, 16, 1963, pp. 251–9

RAMAT RACHEL (Israel) Israelite citadel: Y. Aharoni, *Archaeology*, 18, 1965, pp. 15–25

SALAMIS (Cyprus) Cypro-Phoenician tumulus burials: V. Karageorghis, *ILN*, Aug. 29 and Sept. 5, 1964

TEL ARAD (Israel) Iron Age levels: Y. Aharoni, *RB*, 71, 3, 1964, pp. 393–6

TELL GATH (Israel) Palestinian Egyptian contacts, *IEJ*, 10, 4, 1960, pp. 193–203

THEBES (Greece) Oriental remains from the Cadmeion: N. Platon, *ILN*, Nov. 28 and Dec. 5, 1964

ZARETHAN (Jordan) Late Bronze Age tombs and metalwork: J. B. Pritchard, *ILN*, March 28, 1964

List of Illustrations

The author and publishers are grateful to the many official bodies, institutions and individuals mentioned below for their assistance in supplying illustration material. Illustrations without acknowledgement are from originals in the archives of Thames and Hudson.

19 Gold votive vase from the temple deposit, Byblos. National Museum, Beirut. Photo Epco

20 Copies of painting from the tomb of Khnumhotep. Beni Hasan. From C.R. Lepsius *Denkmäler aus Ägypten und Äthiopien*, 1849–1859, vol. 2, Taf. 133

21 Early second millennium obelisk temple, Byblos. Photo Richard Dormer

22 Twelfth-dynasty statue of User from Knossos. Herakleion Museum

23 Fragment of a wall-painting from Mari. Louvre. Photo Eileen Tweedy

24 Silver-fluted 'teapot' from the tomb of Abi-shemu, Byblos, National Museum, Beirut. Photo courtesy of the Director General, Service des Antiquités, Lebanon

25 Alabastron lid with name of Hyksos king Khian, from Knossos. Herakleion Museum

26 Hyksos spiked bit from Tell el-Ajjul. Archaeological Museum, Jerusalem. Photo courtesy of the Director

27 Tuthmosis III smiting Syrians, seventh pylon at Karnak. Photo Max Hirmer

28 Festival Hall of Tuthmosis III, Karnak, from the south-east. Photo Peter Clayton

29 Mitannian cylinder seal from Tell Atchana. Drawn by Hubert Pepper

30 Cylinder seal from Tripoli, Lebanon. Private collection. After Seyrig

31 Mitannian cylinder seal. Staatliche Museen, Berlin. Photo Staatliche Museen

32 Mitannian cylinder seal. British Museum. Photo courtesy of the Trustees of the British Museum

33 Bronze statuette of a vassal Mitannian prince, from Egypt. Cairo Museum. Photo courtesy of the Director General, Service des Antiquités, Cairo

34 White magnesite statue of King Idrimi of Alalakh, from Tell Atchana. British Museum. Photo John Freeman

35 Panel with battle scene from a painted casket found in the tomb of Tut-ankh-amun at Thebes. Cairo Museum

36 Levantine traders in Egypt. Reconstruction painting by Gaynor Chapman

37 Wall-painting of Canaanite traders from tomb 162, Kenamun, at Thebes. Drawn by N. de G. Davies. Courtesy of the Egypt Exploration Society

38 Chariot from the tomb of Amenophis III at Thebes, Archaeological Museum, Florence. Photo Alinari

39 Blue faience rhyton from Citium. Cyprus Museum. Photo courtesy of Dr V. Karageorghis, Cypriot Department of Antiquities

40 Levantine vessels from Egypt. Black flask and spindle bottle from Sidmant; oil horn from a tomb at Kurneh, Thebes. Royal Scottish Museum, Edinburgh. Photo Tom Scott

41 Painting from the tomb of Senmut, Thebes. Copy by Nina M. Davies. Photo courtesy of the Oriental Institute, University of Chicago

42 Wall-painting of Syrian tribute bearers from the tomb of Sobekhotep, Thebes. British Museum. Photo courtesy of the Trustees of the British Museum

43 Bound Canaanite as the handle of a walking-stick, from the tomb of

Tut-ankh-amun at Thebes. Cairo Museum. Photo Griffith Institute, Ashmolean Museum

44 Amenophis III marriage scarab from Ras Shamra. After Schaeffer

45 Niqmadu 'marriage vase' from Ras Shamra. Photo courtesy of Professor C.F.A. Schaeffer

46 Cretan tribute of cups and ingots, from a wall-painting in the tomb of Rekhmire, Thebes. Photo Peter Clayton

47 Ox-hide ingot from Cape Gelidonya wreck. Photo courtesy of the University of Pennsylvania Museum

48 Corroded ingots recovered from the Cape Gelidonya wreck. Photo courtesy of Miss J. du Plat Taylor

49 Ivory game-box with pieces, and two mirror handles, from Enkomi, Cyprus. British Museum. Photo Eileen Tweedy

50 Clay tablet inscribed in Cypro-Minoan script, from Ras Shamra. After Schaeffer

51 Finds from a Mycenaean tomb at Perati, Attica. After *Archäologischer Anzeiger*

52 Wooden cup in the form of a woman's head from Egypt. Burrell Collection, Glasgow City Museum and Art Gallery

53 Openwork plaque of a 'Bes' figure, from Megiddo. Oriental Institute, University of Chicago. Photo courtesy of the Oriental Institute

54 Ivory lid of an unguent box from Ras Shamra. Louvre. Photo Maurice Chuzeville

55 Ivory winged griffin plaque, from Megiddo. Oriental Institute, University of Chicago. Photo courtesy of the Oriental Institute

56 Incised ivory plaque with scene of Canaanite king and captives, from Megiddo. Oriental Institute, University of Chicago. Photo courtesy of the Oriental Institute

57, 59 Inner and outer faces of an ivory panel from the royal bed in the palace at Ras Shamra. Damascus Museum. Photo courtesy of the Director of Antiquities of the Syrian Arab Republic

58 Ivory oliphant from Ras Shamra. Damascus Museum. Photo courtesy of the Director of Antiquities of the Syrian Arab Republic

60 Ivory head of a queen from Ras Shamra. Damascus Museum. Photo courtesy of the Director of Antiquities of the Syrian Arab Republic

61 Gold bowl in repoussé work with mythical animals from Ras Shamra. Aleppo Museum. Photo courtesy of the Director of Antiquities of the Syrian Arab Republic

62 Gold bowl with hunting scenes, from Ras Shamra. Louvre. Photo Archives

63 Bronze plaque of a Canaanite dignitary, from the temple at Hazor. After Yadin

64 Relief of an Egyptian sea battle from the temple of Medinet Habu, Thebes

65 Ox-hide ingot with foundry mark from Cape Gelidonya wreck. Photo courtesy of the University of Pennsylvania Museum

66 Ox-hide ingot from Serra Ilixi, Sardinia. Photo courtesy of Professor C. Zervos

67 Ox-hide ingot with trident mark from Hagia Triada. Herakleion Museum, Crete. Drawn by Hubert J. Pepper

68 Bronze cauldron stand with man carrying ox-hide ingot, from Curium, Cyprus. British Museum. Photo courtesy of the Trustees of the British Museum

69 Bronze wheeled cauldron stand with sphinxes from Larnaka, Cyprus. Staatliche Museen, Berlin. Photo courtesy of the Director

70 Bronze wheeled cauldron stand with musicians. British Museum. Photo courtesy of the Trustees of the British Museum

71 Ivory openwork plaque of a Canaanite maiden, from Megiddo. Oriental Institute, University of Chicago. Photo courtesy of the Oriental Institute

72 Ivory figurine in high relief from Megiddo. Oriental Institute, University of Chicago. Photo courtesy of the Oriental Institute

73 Ivory comb with animal combat, from Megiddo. Palestine Archaeological Museum. Photo courtesy of the Director

74 Box carved from a single piece of ivory with lions and sphinxes, from Megiddo. Palestine Archaeological Museum. Photo courtesy of the Director

75 Faience tiles depicting Asiatics, from Medinet Habu, Thebes. Boston Museum of Fine Arts

76 Foreign prisoners of Ramesses III, Medinet Habu, Thebes. Photo courtesy of the Oriental Institute, University of Chicago

77 Sword with the cartouche of Merneptah, from Ras Shamra. Damascus Museum. Photo courtesy of Professor C.F.A. Schaeffer

78 Late Bronze Age temple in Area H at Hazor looking north. Photo courtesy of Professor Y. Yadin

79 Proto-Aeolic capital, from Hazor. Photo courtesy of the Oriental Institute, University of Chicago

80 Ivory pyxis in Syrian style, from Nimrud. British Museum. Photo courtesy of the Trustees of the British Museum

81 Votive limestone stele in the form of a volute capital, from Golgoi, Cyprus. Metropolitan Museum of Art, New York

82 Incense stand and strainer jug from Tel Amal. Drawn by Gillian Jones

83 Inscribed sherd from Tell Qasile. Museum Haaretz, Tel Aviv. Photo Prior

84 Ivory plaque with Egyptian motifs, from Nimrud. British Museum. Photo courtesy of Professor M.E.L. Mallowan and the Trustees of the British Museum

85 Openwork ivory cow and calf, from Arslan Tash, Syria. Louvre. Photo Archives

86 Openwork ivory figure of a sphinx, from Arslan Tash, Syria. Metropolitan Museum of Art, New York, Near Eastern Department, Fletcher Fund

87 Inlaid ivory plaque of a lion devouring a boy, from Nimrud. British Museum. Courtesy of Professor M.E.L. Mallowan. Photo Eileen Tweedy

88 Ivory plaque with a goddess, from Nimrud. Iraq Museum. Baghdad. Photo courtesy of Professor M.E.L. Mallowan and the British School of Archaeology in Iraq

89 Ivory panel with god and fruits from Nimrud. Photo courtesy of Professor M.E.L. Mallowan and the British School of Archaeology in Iraq

90 Ivory plaque with 'woman at the window', from Nimrud. British Museum. Courtesy of the Trustees of the British Museum

91 Ivory plaque with *djed* pillar and goddesses, from Samaria. Palestine Archaeological Museum. Photo courtesy of the Director

92 Ivory medallion with Horus on a lotus, from Samaria. Palestine Archaeological Museum. Photo courtesy of the Director

93 Openwork plaque with winged 'cherub' sphinx, from Samaria. Palestine Archaeological Museum. Photo courtesy of the Director

94 Ivory openwork plaque with a lion in a lily grove, from Nimrud. British Museum. Courtesy of Professor M.E.L. Mallowan. Photo Eileen Tweedy

95 Ivory plaque of Assyrian workmanship, from the Ziwiyeh treasure. Teheran Archaeological Museum. Photo Josephine Powell

96 Carved ivory with Iranian theme, from the Ziwiyeh treasure. Teheran Archaeological Museum. Photo Josephine Powell

97 'Caryatid' figure from the Tell Halaf palace. Staatliche Museen, Berlin

98 Reconstruction of the palace façade from Tell Halaf. Staatliche Museen, Berlin. Photo Marburg

99 Grey steatite 'pipe bowl', from Carchemish. British Museum. Photo John Freeman

100 Bronze bowl from Nimrud. British Museum. Photo courtesy of the Trustees of the British Museum

101 Painted jug from Citium, Cyprus. Ashmolean Museum. Photo Eileen Tweedy

102 Five jugs from Cyprus. Metropolitan Museum of Art, New York

103 Phoenician glass beads from Cyprus. Royal Scottish Museum, Edinburgh. Photo Tom Scott

104 Gold sceptre inlaid with blue and white pastes, from Curium, Cyprus. Cyprus Museum, Nicosia

105 Scent-bottle of Phoenician glass from Cyprus. Metropolitan Museum of Art, New York

106 Rhodian pottery. Drawn by Gillian Jones after Riis and Naveh

107 Bronze Urartian tripod-cauldron from Altintepe. Ankara Museum. Photo courtesy of Dr R.D. Barnett

108 Phoenician princess at her toilet. Reconstruction painting by Gaynor Chapman

109 Map of the eastern Mediterranean. Drawn by Gillian Jones

110 Philistine cult and libation vessels from Ashdod. Drawn by Gillian Jones after Dothan

111 Phoenician pottery from Achzib. Drawn by Gillian Jones

112 Phoenician gold crowns. Walters Art Gallery, Baltimore. Photo Walters Art Gallery

113 Gold ornament depicting Phoenician shrine. Ashmolean Museum, Oxford. Photo Ashmolean Museum

114 Terracotta statuette of a woman, possibly from Idalium, Cyprus. Louvre. Photo Maurice Chuzeville

115 Phoenician inscription from Nora, Cape Pula, Sardinia. Cagliari Museum, Sardinia. Photo courtesy of the Soprintendenza alle Antichità, Cagliari

116 Gold pendant from Carthage with Punic inscription. Lavigerie Museum, Carthage. Drawn by Marion Cox after *Cat. Mus. Lavigerie*

117 Cinerary urn and painted pottery from the Tanit precinct, Carthage. Alaoui Museum, Tunis. Drawn by Hubert Pepper

118 Precinct of Tanit, Carthage. Photo courtesy the Director, Alaoui Museum, Tunis

119 Urns and stelae of the second stratum in the precinct of Tanit, Carthage. Photo courtesy of Dr D.B. Harden

120 Grotesque pottery mask from Tharros, Sardinia. British Museum. Photo courtesy of the Trustees of the British Museum

121 Silver shekel of Tyre, *c.* 460 BC. Obv., dolphin; rev., owl. British Museum. Photo Peter Clayton

122 Map of the Phoenician colonies in the Western Mediterranean. Drawn by Gillian Jones

123 Silver drinking bowl from the Bernardini tomb, Praeneste, Italy. Museo Preistorico L. Pigorini. Photo courtesy Soprintendenza alle Antichità

124 Silver bowl from Amathus, Cyprus. British Museum. Drawn by Marion Cox after Perrot and Chipiez

125 Marble alabastron of Cypro-Phoenician design from Vulci. British Museum. Photo courtesy of the Trustees of the British Museum

126 Silver bowl with mixed art motifs, from Idalium, Cyprus. Louvre. Photo Maurice Chuzeville

127 Detail of a Phoenician silver bowl. Cleveland Museum of Art. J.H. Wade collection

128 Gold belt-end from Aliseda, Spain. Museo Arqueologico Nacional, Madrid. Photo Museo Arqueologico

129 Part of the gold treasure from El Carambolo, Spain. Archaeological Museum, Seville. Photo courtesy of Professor J. de Mata Carriazo

130 Bone comb from Carmona, Spain. Hispanic Society of America, New York

131 Ivory panel from a box, from Carmona, Spain. Hispanic Society of America, New York

132 Bronze jug of Phoenician type. Metropolitan Museum of Art, Pulitzer Bequest Fund

133 Painted tankard from Ras Shamra. Drawn by the author after Schaeffer

134 Cuneiform alphabetic tablet from Ras Shamra. After Diringer

135 Baked clay tablet from Tell Taanach. Drawn by the author after Hillers

136 Development of the linear alphabet. After Albright

137 Phoenician inscription from Ahiram sarcophagus. After Montet

138 Sarcophagus of Ahiram, from his tomb at Byblos. National Museum, Beirut. Photo courtesy of the Director General, Service des Antiquités, Lebanon

139 Inscribed dagger from Lachish. Palestine Archaeological Museum. Photo courtesy of the Director

Index

Numbers in italics refer to the illustrations